ELISHA DAVIDSON ▽

and the Letters of Fire

Part One of a Trilogy

by

M.R. ATTAR

MENORAH
B O O K S

HONG KONG · JERUSALEM · USA

Elisha Davidson & the Letters of Fire

Published by MENORAH BOOKS LIMITED

Copyright © September 2014, M. Rhonda Attar

EDITING: Chaim Natan Firszt, Ashirah Yosefah
COVER DESIGN: Gal Narunsky
TYPOGRAPHY & LAYOUT: Gal Narunsky
PRINTER: Old City Press, Jerusalem

INFORMATION AND INQUIRIES: administrator@menorah-books.com

ISBN: 978-1-940516-20-2

FOR ORDERS:
INTERNET: www.menorah-books.com
EMAIL: orders@menorah-books.com

To my mother, Z"L, who made a new day
something wonderful to look forward to.
To my father, Z"L, who made me acutely aware that each day
might behold a separate and mysterious reality.
To my husband Meir, who taught me how to make a day
truly meaningful.
To my children Arielle, Moriah and Sivan, who fill my day
with living, giving and receiving.
And above all, to the Master of the Universe,
in Whose infinite compassion I receive a new day.

There's a saying that the greatest sparks can only come into the world using the *back* door.

CHAPTER 1

The New Moon of Tammuz

The New Moon of the month of Tammuz fell on Sunday, June 25th. It wasn't a very favorable month on the Hebrew calendar. The only month considered worse was Av, and it was the one to follow. But that thought never occurred to Elisha Davidson. He was running home through the Old City streets of Jerusalem after the 'accident', and the only image in his mind was of how Professor Bezalel was staring so strangely at his face before it happened. His only hope at the time was that no one else had noticed.

The day had started off with no hint of an impending disaster. It was just another regular day at the North Temple Mount Academy. The sun was shining more brightly than usual through the stained glass windows of the assembly hall, and after singing praises for the New Moon, Elisha and his classmates had dutifully filed into their sixth grade classroom and waited in their assigned seats for the tidal wave of energy that would signal the entrance of their teacher, Professor Daniel Bezalel.

Any unfamiliar onlooker, however, would have been totally alarmed to see the Professor enter the classroom. The scholarly 38-year old was a shadow of a man, a towering skeleton with raven black hair that fell limply over chiseled features that were as colorless as a lifeless statue. Oddly enough, his deathlike aura didn't entirely disguise his magnificence. In fact, if his face had the slightest sign of good health, it would have been fought over by every aspiring artist as the model for their masterpiece. But, unfortunately, he had spent well over ten years giving off the appearance that he was in the very last stages of a terminal disease.

The usual label of 'teacher' was also misleading, because Professor Bezalel was never satisfied for his class to simply 'learn' about his particular subject of *Vayikra*, or specifically, the Temple. He was so obsessed with it that he expected all of his students to see it, touch it, and breathe in its air, even though it had been in ruins for thousands of years. Outside the school's doors, he was the Director of the Temple Antiquities Museum in Jerusalem, and outside of the country, it was Sir Daniel Bezalel, Professor of Theoretical Physics at the University of Cambridge. It was only in a very small and closed circle that Professor Bezalel was also cryptically known as a *Mekubal*, a 'Master' of the mystical and ancient teachings. But all those titles were meaningless in the North Temple Mount classrooms. Here he was simply a living legend.

But on this Sunday, June 25th, everyone had clear proof that Professor Bezalel was a regular human being after all. He was sweating profusely, which wasn't unusual for him, as he held a furled parchment scroll raised high in one hand. With the other, he was pointing to the whiteboard which had a colorful diagram of the *Choshen*, the mysterious breastplate worn thousands of years ago by the High Priest that was used as an oracle in the Temple. It had twelve different large and sparkling precious gems, arranged in four rows, each engraved with the name of a tribe of Israel in ancient Hebrew script. Elisha's sixth grade class had studied the Chosen in such meticulous detail that most of the students could have drawn one in their sleep, *except* for one all-important detail. The Choshen only turned into an oracle when the mystifying *Urim V'Tumim* were placed inside of it. But since no one on the planet, including Professor Bezalel, had any idea what they were, they could at least rest assured that it wouldn't turn up on their upcoming final exam either.

Professor Bezalel was at the end of his Choshen review drill.

"Perfect . . . Powerful . . . En-*light*-enment!"

For effect, he banged the whiteboard three times. Then he singled out Josh Kohen in the last row on the right and asked, "Could this still possibly look like some kind of magical amulet to you?"

Elisha couldn't help thinking that it still did.

Professor Bezalel didn't wait for an answer. He breathed in a long deep breath which never seemed to come out and was in a wide-eyed fervor when he said, "Absurd! The real *power* is in the l·e·t·t·e·r·s themselves! The mathematical, numerical, and atomic calculations derived from arranging these letters." He lovingly traced the letters on the whiteboard. "*Forget* what you thought you knew about the Hebrew alphabet! These l·e·t·t·e·r·s are not just text, they're not just numbers, they're NOT just a means of communication—they are *symbols* and each and every one possesses its own world of extraordinary powers!" He paused meaningfully and then scanned every face in the classroom, "And when they are joined together in the right sequential formulas, they have the potential power for much, *much* more than that . . . They can also form *The Name*."

An intense hush hovered over the classroom. Elisha sat quietly, anxiously absorbing every word, but he also knew that he'd have to be a well-trained Chamber Seven graduate before he could ever really understand that awesome power.

In the full weight of the suspenseful silence, Professor Bezalel slowly turned to face the right hand side of the class where he had seated all the students with priestly lineage, but then suddenly he made a whiplash movement in Elisha's direction and then fixed his eyes on Elisha's face in complete bewilderment. He gave a burning glare, a deep and long stare, scorching, steady and relentless, straight into Elisha's eyes. And that's when it happened.

In front of the whole class, the towering professor had an awkward spasm and collapsed with one great shake and quiver onto the floor. The most unfortunate part was that his head collided with the corner of the desk with a thick thud, and it only took seconds for the shocked class to see that he was lying crumpled and motionless, and worse, there was actually blood spurting out of him, forming a pool of crimson red as it flooded onto the white marble floor.

The screams of the panicked students quickly reached the alert ears of Principal Oholiov, who naturally, was always in the habit of patrolling the hallways.

Elisha couldn't move or make a sound. He was transfixed to his seat just staring in horror at the unconscious boney body on the floor that looked so much smaller now. In a sickly way it reminded him of how big spiders looked after you stepped on them. They were always so much tinier once they were crushed. Hysteria ensued all around him, and the school nurse was rushed to the scene. With growing nausea, Elisha continued to gaze at the ever-growing puddle of blood. It was going to reach his sneakers any second now . . . any second. It was Principal Oholiov's booming bass voice that jolted Elisha out of his frozen state.

"You, yes you, Davidson!" he shouted with his usual tone of authority, "OUT. Now!" he ordered while pointing sharply to the door.

Elisha was quick once he found his feet and thankful that the principal had saved him from watching the real-life nightmare close-up. The principal continued calling out by name those lingerers who held a sickly fascination for the disaster. In seconds, they were all herded through the vaulted stone archway corridors of the school.

Elisha heard the hyper conversation of his classmates buzzing all around him.

"My brother always said that he looks like a skeleton because he fasts all the time."

"I heard he actually *is* half-dead."

"Yeah, I heard that too and that's how he knows the secrets of the Temple."

Elisha was in a numb, detached state with his own thoughts. He knew they were being ridiculous, because his father had told him that Professor Bezalel suffered from a metabolic disease, whatever that was, but at that moment he wasn't even sure if he knew how to speak anymore.

When Elisha's class entered the cavernous auditorium, Mrs. Moran, the school's social worker, was already raising her voice over the screeching microphone feedback. For some reason, the Eternal Lamp was out of whack and flickering wildly over her head, casting a dizzying kaleidoscope of spots onto her face.

"Everyone sit down and calm down," she repeated over and over in frustration. Meanwhile, she fumbled helplessly with the lighting panel as if that would do something, but, no one offered her any help.

No one was listening to her either. She certainly wasn't sitting down and definitely wasn't calm. Her grating voice and strobe-like face rattled on, and threatened, "We're not going to talk about this until everyone sits down and calms down!"

Elisha groaned. Why in the world did she think that 'talking' about something they needed to block out forever was some kind of incentive to be quiet? He took a seat in the far back and that's when his numbed mind started working furiously overtime. Couldn't he have been the one to save him? How come he didn't just jump up quickly from his desk in those split seconds and grab the falling giant? Why didn't he realize something was wrong when Professor Bezalel gave him that weird stare? And he was seeing it over and over again in his mind, and each time he had been the hero and saved the thankful professor from that most dangerous of weapons, the desk corner.

Principal Ezra Oholiov was studying every nuance and detail of the empty classroom. He was missing something vital and he was the only one that might ever be able to spot it before it was gone. He wasn't a Chamber graduate himself, so he had limited tools to figure out how the incomprehensible had happened to Professor Bezalel, but he certainly knew enough of the basics to be able to detect any sort of foul play. At least, he hoped he did. He was sure that the kids weren't involved. How could they have been? None of them had been initiated *yet* into the Chambers Program.

He checked the walls, windows, floor, and ceiling for the tenth time. Nothing. He went through every book and piece of paper. Nothing. This particular classroom was also a new addition, and it had never even housed any of the school's ancient manuscripts, scrolls or amulets. He erased the whiteboard with Professor Bezalel's Choshen diagram. It was standard sixth grade curriculum fare and not relevant. He checked the seating arrangements, along with a diagram of the kids' names which he had removed from his personal safe. There were three that had Professor Bezalel's mark for special Chamber initiation. He saw that he was sitting in one of the marked seats. He checked again. It belonged to Elisha Davidson. That was definitely an absurd choice. He was the youngest student in the class, and despite better judgment, Ezra had succumbed to the father's pressure to allow him to start school early. It was still a mistake in his opinion. The kid certainly didn't show that he had inherited any of his father's genius. He probably was closest to Professor Bezalel when it happened. Ezra made a mental note of the other two names that were marked. Now those were more interesting choices.

As he got up, he reached for the furled scroll that was on the desk. He had remembered that it was covered in blood when he had come into the classroom. It had been on the floor right next to Professor Bezalel's head. Someone had apparently cleaned it. It was still wet and smelled like floor cleaner. The carefully handwritten Ashurite script was scoured away in places. Ezra couldn't even fathom the IQ of the genius who had done it, and then he remembered what they were paying the new cleaning help. He put the scroll carefully under his arm, intent on giving it a proper burial as soon as he could.

He left the classroom feeling entirely frustrated, but made sure to remove the scribed parchment that was affixed to the doorway. It was rolled up and hidden in a small hand-painted encasement that had the usual acronym 'Guardian of the Doors of Israel'. He would urgently have it checked to see if there was even the slightest sign of defect in the indelible ink inscriptions. He unrolled the miniature scroll. It was entirely blank. The 15 verses from *Devarim* were not even there! That was entirely impossible, but, he couldn't spend any more time with his own investigation; he urgently needed to deal with the sixth graders and then get to the hospital.

With a dull sense of disorientation, Elisha realized that Mrs. Moran had finally overcome the awesome task of quieting the room. With the newly gained silence and her self-confidence restored, she was slightly calmer.

"Now that's so much better, isn't it?" she sighed. "Okay, who would like to tell me exactly what happened?"

Big mistake, thought Elisha, and as he expected, the generous volunteer was Avshalom, who ran up and unceremoniously grabbed the microphone right out of a flustered Mrs. Moran's hands. He was the class tyrant, and at this moment, his prime concern was to hear his nasty voice amplified.

"Testing 1, 2, 3," he repeated and shouted at close range right into the mike.

The entire auditorium had to block their ears so they wouldn't be deafened by his loud spitting noises combined with the shrieking feedback. Mrs. Moran tried pitifully to regain control of the microphone with some of her own shrieking, but it was useless. It took Principal Oholiov's entrance through the back door to immediately restore order and instantly achieve pin drop silence. His voice boomed across the auditorium.

"Do you have something to say, Avshalom?"

Despite his repulsion, Elisha found himself paying very careful attention. He needed to know if Avshalom was going to mention anything about him.

"I saw the whole thing," he boasted in an arrogant tone (as if no one else did). "He was talking and talking and sweating, like he always does, and then he stared into thin air and flopped to the floor, and WHACK, his head smashed right into his own desk, just like this."

Avshalom acted out the movements with clown-like gusto and quickly performed three more re-enactments. He would have done it a fourth time if Principal Oholiov hadn't held up his hand and firmly said, "Enough!" There was no doubt that Avshalom was savoring the whole disaster along with the limelight, and Elisha's stomach churned in disgust. On the other hand, he was so relieved to hear those same words, 'stared into thin air'. But, for some strange reason, it wasn't enough that Avshalom hadn't noticed, Elisha had, and now a strange thought gnawed at the back of his mind. *He remembered staring weirdly at Professor Bezalel first.* Elisha blocked out the memory, but his whole body still felt sickened by an inexplicable guilt.

After some convincing, Principal Oholiov decided to send the class home a whole hour early, since according to Mrs. Moran they had all 'undergone a trauma', especially herself.

Needing no microphone, Principal Oholiov raised his hands to quiet the room and then announced, "I've just been informed that Professor Bezalel is in the good hands of the talented doctors at Mount Scopus Hospital. Let's all take a moment to say a prayer for his speedy recovery and then you may go."

The prayer moment lasted five seconds before the stampede of students bounded out of the room. Elisha felt catapulted free. He darted out of the school with lightning speed and ran home through the narrow Jerusalem alleyways as if a madman was chasing him.

The windowless room was roughly circular. The ceiling was low. Its stones were darker black than any dungeon's. They were also cool and gave off the heady scent of water that ran deeply underground. It was the perfect place to picture infinity, to imagine the depth of the earth and beyond the earth, the height of the sky and beyond the sky, the height of the universe and beyond the universe. It was the perfect place to imagine infinite time—never-ending time in the past and never-ending time in the future.

The point of infinity needed to be pictured clearly. It was endlessly large and infinitely small, and it didn't have a shape, and it didn't actually exist in space or time. But, the point was there. When you could envision the point of infinity, then you could at least begin. If you couldn't, then there was nothing more for you to do, because the *Sephirot* are infinite and because The Timeless Reality is Infinite.

She could see the point right away. She understood. Everyone else couldn't. In a way, she knew they were born blind. She opened her eyes and spoke light into the room. She wondered what she could do to the stone walls to make them match her new pink and purple pillow set. Should she cover them with fish? Maybe grass? It was things like these that she had a hard time figuring out.

The stone pathways were already heated to oven temperatures in the midday summer sun. By the time Elisha had reached the shady olive tree courtyard of his home, there wasn't a part on his body that wasn't sticky with sweat, and he could see his chest pounding through his T-shirt. He inadvertently slammed the dark green wrought-iron front gate loud enough to attract the entire neighborhood's attention. But, he was greeted by nothing. Where was his family? All the rooms in the house were empty. He wondered if they had already heard about Professor Bezalel, and maybe they had rushed out to the hospital or worse . . . a funeral. It took the sudden loud crashing sound from the back of the house for Elisha to remember . . . and in an instant!

It was renovation day at the Davidson's. The small bathroom in their typical apartment at 26 Gates Street was about to double in size, but renovating anything in the Old City was extremely tricky. Most of the houses were new, but everything was built over ancient foundations dating back thousands of years, which meant that you never knew exactly what you'd find when you broke through the extremely thick Jerusalem stone walls. Most people didn't want to find anything of archaeological importance because that, of course, would end up turning their homes into State museums. But as for 26 Gates Street, the municipality and architect had agreed that there was a little extra space with absolutely no historical value whatsoever behind the Davidson's family bathroom.

The realization that it was renovation day was a huge relief. It was so boring and comfortably normal that Elisha felt the terrible burden of the day lighten a little. He darted towards the scene of the small but overcrowded construction site until he ran full force into his mother's outstretched seatbelt arm blocking the hallway. For the second time in one day, he was being ordered out.

"Watch OUT. *Out of the way*!" Tamar Davidson's voice rang with urgency.

But Elisha was so desperate for attention, he could easily block out the busy scene in front of him. He yelled out, but halfway into his sentence, the wall that was slated to go came down with a huge crash and rumble. The noise and dust were overwhelming, and Elisha's mother gasped and fanned the front of her face, all the while moving Elisha out of harm's way. It only took a split second for the power tools to screech and buzz again. The loud racket made concentrating on anything else impossible. It was then that the throbbing in Elisha's chest moved up into his head. He could see his father emerging from the new crevice looking utterly satisfied with the mess and destruction as if it was some fascinating Do-It-Yourself science project. His father didn't even notice him. It was in a moment of utter frustration, that he felt his mother's strong hand leading him out of the chaos.

In the safety of the clean and noiseless kitchen, Elisha was surprised that you could actually hear yourself speak. He practically choked on his own words from the speed of getting the Professor Bezalel story out of his mouth. His mother was quicker. In seconds, she had updated his father and had pulled him from the wreckage.

Jessie Davidson seemed relatively unaware that he was coated from head to toe in white dust. He was more aggravated at the unexpected distraction. He wiped the dust off his glasses and started calling Principal Oholiov on his phone, while pacing restlessly within the small confines of the kitchen. He was just about to open his mouth when everyone was physically jolted in their places. A split second later there was a deafening cracking sound, as if they had just been hit by a thunderous lightning bolt, and the windows were rattling violently.

Elisha's mother immediately said, "*That* was a *huge* sonic boom!" but she was looking right at her husband and asking it rather than stating it.

It wasn't unusual in the small Israeli air space to have F-15 and F-16 fighter planes breaking the sound barrier during their training maneuvers. People were used to it. The problem was that the sound of a terrorist bombing wasn't too different.

Elisha's father was studying something on his phone and muttered, "I'm sure it was just a sonic boom," and then he completed the call and reached for the radio, tuning it to a news station.

Elisha carefully followed his father's one-sided conversation with the principal, while hanging on to every expression and "I see."

"It's the wildest thing," said his father while hitting

'end' on the call. He frowned as he digested the distressing news. It was only his wife's firm and impatient, "WELL?" that reminded him there were other people to share information with.

"No, don't worry." He turned to Elisha and said loudly, "He's alive," as if Elisha had grossly exaggerated the situation. "In fact, he's already regained consciousness, but the problem seems to be that he has amnesia on top of whatever medical condition triggered the whole incident." His face was puzzled and very troubled.

Elisha thought that was a rather strong reaction for his usually unemotional father, but then he remembered that Professor Bezalel and his father were working on some kind of important book together. And books were *always* his father's number one priority.

As for Elisha, he felt like he was swallowing for the first time since it had happened. The black cloud that was lurking in his mind suddenly lifted. He hadn't killed him. His father had said so. It was only this amnesia bit, which didn't sound so bad, right? Elisha blurted out anxiously, "What kind of amnesia does he have?"

His father looked at him with frustrated impatience. "What *kind*? The kind where you lose your memory, Elisha. What do you mean what *kind*?"

Another massive sonic boom rattled the house. They usually did come in twos. The radio station droned on in the background without any urgency in the newscaster's voice. That meant that Professor Bezalel still held first place for disaster of the day. Elisha could tell that his father wanted to focus on the news, but asked anyway, "I mean does he have the kind that goes away right away or is it forever?"

"I have no idea," he snapped.

Elisha's mother took over, throwing a hostile glare at his father, but her own voice sounded too sugar-coated to Elisha. "Oh, it's nothing. Things like that almost *always* happen after a head injury." She put her arm over Elisha's shoulder and walked him to the kitchen table thinking out loud. "His poor family, though. He probably doesn't recognize any of them right now. That's so strange to think about." She absent-mindedly opened the fridge and asked over her shoulder, "You want cereal for lunch?" Without waiting for him to say yes, she took out the milk and set down a box, bowl and spoon.

Elisha absorbed her words. What if Professor Bezalel never recovered? That would mean there actually wouldn't be a Professor Bezalel anymore as far as they knew him. *Wasn't that a kind of death if you thought about it too much?* He could feel his eyes silently growing wide with alarm. His mother noticed and sent him to his room to "relax and unwind" until suppertime, while his parents went back to the currently much more urgent and important task of supervising the construction.

As if reading his mind, his father added, "Now don't you dare go telling Saba Gabriel about any of this. He doesn't need to know."

The third sonic boom was so earsplitting that Elisha felt his insides had come out. His cereal had also plopped out of his bowl in every direction.

Jessie Davidson ran outside and searched the cloudless sky. He then saw one of the construction workers unloading a cart of cinder blocks. He yelled out, "*Do these sonic booms interfere with your work?*"

The man looked blankly at him and then seemed pleased at the welcomed opportunity to stop working all together. He looked down at his hands, set down one

of the cinder blocks and sat on it. Jessie figured he was
about to get a complicated explanation on the effects of
sonic booms during construction, but instead the worker
just asked, "What sonic booms?"

In seconds, Elisha's father was back in the house and
rushing toward the bathroom yelling, "It's the workers!
You can't leave them for a second! *WHAT* in the world
are they doing in there?"

The answer was nothing. They were all having yet
another coffee break. The workers exchanged knowing
looks at Mr. Davidson's stressed face. It was obviously this
guy's first taste of hands-on construction. Okay, so they
had used too many power tools at once and it overloaded
the circuitry, but geez, you'd think they had blown the
whole house up. One of the workers sighed sorrowfully
and shook his head. You could just tell that Davidson
was the type that had his wife changing the light bulbs.

Deported to his room, Elisha laid on his comfortable bed with an open book, but there was too much
action going on. Elisha felt he was contracting one of his
mother's migraines, along with amnesia. He threw the
book to the side and stared at the ceiling. He guessed it
went without saying that there wouldn't be a Chamber
One summer camp this year. It was supposed to start in
two and a half weeks, and he had been registered since
birth. He had been looking forward to it since the first
grade. Everyone knew that it was the most amazing thing
you could ever do. Yet no one dared to talk about what
went on, and that was a main part of the fascination.
There were seven Chambers, and they were all held in the
'Foundation Vault', a highly restricted area somewhere
near the Temple's Western Wall Tunnels and underneath
the site of Solomon's ancient Temple. Initiates could only

enter it accompanied by Professor Bezalel. Another uncomfortable pang hit his chest with a flash of the haunting
stare and collapse. How was he supposed to relax? Even
with the door of his room shut tight, he could still feel
the vibrations and hear the spine-shivering noises of the
power tools. It was a major relief to finally hear it stop
some two hours later, and Elisha took that as his cue to
rejoin the living.

There was a noisy mechanical humming in the sterile
room where Rebecca's husband lay limp in a drug-induced
sleep. She was standing in the corner, trying to hide her
sobbing face by pretending to study the ugly vinyl curtains
that hung over the windows of the fluorescent-lit hospital
room, but it didn't do much to hide her shaking body.

Principal Ezra Oholiov noticed it the minute he
walked in, and he put his hand gently on her shoulder.
He didn't expect it would trigger her to turn around so
wildly. Her pretty face was red and swollen from crying,
but the anger in her eyes was vivid and aflame, and her
hands were shaking in fury at her sides.

"Don't you look at me like you don't know why this
is happening," she hissed through her gritted teeth.

Ezra misread her anger and tried to offer her comfort
with a hug. She immediately threw her brother's hands
off with such force that even he was shocked.

"Rebecca, *stop it*!" he demanded as all his tenderness
dissipated. His voice had a hard edge to it now. "You're
doing nothing at *all* to help the situation by acting like
this."

"*Yes, but you did it, you did it!*" she whimpered, and then fell into a chair crying like the little sister he always remembered.

It was a pool of grief. He didn't know what she was talking about, but his heart still ached for her, until she started speaking again with a voice full of rage.

"It's because of those kids, Ezra. *You* know it. It's because of what you did to all those kids in the Chambers that Daniel doesn't even know his own name! Look at him!" She pointed an accusatory finger at the hospital bed, "*And that's why this happened!*" She locked her eyes directly onto her brother's and dared him to refute what she said.

Ezra Oholiov was more than disturbed. His brother-in-law had chosen a poor confidante in his sister. If she thought she knew, then he urgently needed her to get the facts straight.

"Stop being absurd! I don't know what you heard, but there were only *two* boys, and it was for their absolute own good."

Rebecca stared at her brother now as if he were a madman. "You're crazy, Ezra, do you realize that? You're crazy, and the really grotesque and nauseating part, and I mean *really* sick, is that you don't even know it!" She mimicked his voice with a scathing high-pitched sarcasm. "Oh, I only wiped away the memory of two boys, that's all, *only* two boys."

He took hold of her arm and forced her to listen. "No. Rebecca, you *don't* understand. We didn't wipe away their *whole* memories!" he said, staring at the unconscious Daniel, "and I'm *not* the one that's crazy, but one of those kids would have been if we hadn't acted. We *saved* their lives by . . . by helping them to forget . . . I mean block out . . . disturbing images. And if we hadn't acted, those two Simon kids would have either been committed or worse . . . they could have even committed suicide."

She tore her hand free when he finished, but she wasn't through. "Oh sure, and then what about Jonathan Marks??" she accused with an intense glare.

Now Ezra was pleasantly surprised. So, she didn't really know. She only had partial information. "Nothing was ever done to '*The Other*'," he answered sharply. He still wasn't going to call Jonathan by any other name after what had happened and especially *not* in this room when it was Daniel who had given Jonathan the new name.

But Rebecca felt a searing determination and continued. "NO. You're lying, and that's why *Jonathan Marks*," she put as much emphasis on his name as possible, "is trying to destroy everything you've worked for." She glared sorrowfully over to the hospital bed that her husband was laying in and then hatefully back at her brother. "You deserve it!"

Ezra stared at her in silence. Rebecca may have been Daniel's dedicated wife, but it was Ezra Oholiov that was his loyal servant and there wasn't a thing that he wasn't prepared to do in order to get Daniel's memory back. He thought about the tiny parchment scroll that was now as blank as Daniel's memory. He was absolutely sure, 100% positive, that there wasn't *any* connection to *those* kids. The most important thing was the work. It needed to continue, and nothing would stop it, especially not a freaking-out, clueless, and spoiled younger sister.

It wasn't a very kind brotherly thought, but at times like these, he couldn't help thinking that Daniel could have done much better for himself than his sister.

The roughly circular room was filled with blackness. There was no natural light in the room. There was no ceiling light or candlelight. It was the perfect place to picture nothingness. Nothingness is what you saw when you used your eyes to look into the back of your head. Nothingness is the number you counted before one. Nothingness was very important and definitely not *nothing*. Because when you were nothing, you were above the laws of nature. If you were nothing, then there wasn't *any*thing in the world that could do something to you. If you were *something*, then you were bound to the laws of nature, because the way things worked in the world was that things that were *something* were always doing things to other *somethings*. You needed to achieve nothingness in order to begin. If you couldn't, then there was nothing more for you to do, because there were ten Sephirot of nothingness.

She had always known nothingness. Wasn't everyone born knowing nothingness? She was surprised to see how *hard* it was for everyone else: they must have always been really *something*.

She changed into absolutely nothing, so that she could change into something else. Maybe an eyebrow or a step? She remembered *The Other*. He was so good at thinking of fun things to turn yourself into. Weren't her ideas also fun? That was the difficult part. She wasn't sure.

When Elisha had finished serving time in his room, he found that he wasn't the only one resurfacing. The minute he got to the living room, he saw that his little sister, Shira, was back in the house, hanging off the bulging hip of Gila, their teenaged neighbor. Gila was in 10th grade, but to Elisha she looked like she was already married with ten kids. She was an extremely large and round girl who bumped into everything and anything in her vicinity. And whenever she babysat at their house, which was every day, she cleared out every single snack where sugar was the first ingredient. Elisha watched from the side as he saw his mother inviting her to stay for supper. He could tell she accepted because she clapped her hands together, shouting, "Goody, goody," for Shira's sake. *Great*, he thought, and couldn't help feeling a nasty cruel streak rising.

The racket was subdued now as the workers were finishing up and carting out wheelbarrow after wheelbarrow of debris and chunks of Jerusalem stone. Gila, as usual, was in harm's way. She was nearly run down by a quickly-exiting wheelbarrow. In an effort to hone his rescue reaction time, Elisha had hurriedly shoved her to the side, but she squealed and fell down anyways.

With the last full load on its way out, the heavyset foreman looked satisfied. He shouted over his shoulder, "Dror, you're the last one out, finish up," and he tossed a set of keys right over Elisha's head.

One of the smallest workers, a dark-tanned Yemenite, made the perfect catch. Elisha hoped the workman wouldn't mind if he looked over his shoulder while he went about his business. He didn't, and he was friendly.

"You know," he said, starting a conversation with

Elisha, "most people wouldn't do renovations during the month of Tammuz."

Elisha politely asked, "Really, why?"

"Well, it's unlucky of course! This *is* the month, you know," Dror said as he wiped a filthy rag across a row of tiles and then threw it into the corner. "The beginning of the end. You know, the destruction of everything—the First Temple, and then the Second one, too. Yup," he arched his back while getting up from his crouched position, "building is just plain bad, bad luck in Tammuz."

"Well, I hope it won't be for us," Elisha added optimistically, while thinking they were soon to be the owners of a cursed bathtub.

Dror locked up a large metal tool box, while puckering up his mouth and twitching it from side to side, "I don't know, I kind of had a strange feeling in there . . . ."

"What do you mean?"

Dror just shrugged his shoulders, "I've got no idea." And with that he grabbed his toolbox, whistled an old tune, and said, "I wish you a *good* New Moon of Tammuz, my young friend. You're going to need it."

As far as Elisha was concerned, Dror couldn't have made an exit sooner. He was desperately curious to explore the 'unlucky' construction site firsthand.

The bathroom looked like a miserable wreck, no sign whatsoever of his mother's impending 'renovation', and two steps into the room, Elisha caught sight of his reflection in the dusty medicine cabinet mirror which had fallen to the floor. As he picked it up, he suddenly felt the urge to stare blankly at himself. He wanted to know what it would feel like to look straight at yourself and know *nothing*. He rubbed some of the gritty surface dust away with his fingertips.

Who are you? You've got no name, no memory, no parents, and no home. Elisha stared at himself until his eyes watered, hoping to erase his entire memory for just a split second, but it was impossible. He saw his all-too-familiar face, the one that his parents, teachers, and strange ladies on the street were always recommending 100 SPF sunscreen for. He saw his sandy stick-straight hair and his way-too-large pale-blue eyes, which everyone said were Saba Gabriel's eyes. Elisha thought they were annoyingly girlish-looking because of his stupid long eye lashes, and people loved to comment on that, too. He was *sure* there had to be some way to trim them, and even though his mother had tons of equipment for these sorts of things, she always refused.

He *knew* unmistakably who he was, but at the same time, he also saw an unmistakable flash coming from behind the broken-down wall. He cocked his head, turned around, and definitely saw the flash again. He quickly slipped into the new narrow hole in the wall, and the glint of something bright was right in front of his eyes. Excitedly, Elisha shouted out through the door as loud as he could for his parents, but could tell by the rushed and frightened way they both arrived that he had overdone it.

"Sorry, it's alright. Look! There's some kind of a shiny stone here or something! It's amazing. Take a look! It's right here!"

The excitement in Elisha's voice got the best of his mother, and Tamar Davidson quickly squeezed past the rocks into the passage. She started smearing the thick dust to the side using Dror's filthy rag, and Elisha could now see that the unrecognizable thing had once been his favorite towel. With each wipe she exposed more and more shiny surface.

"Well, what in the world is it?" she said aloud with wonder.

Elisha's father traded places with his mother in the narrow new extension and stared. He was speechless for a second, but then went right for the straight, hands-on method. "Well, let's see if we can move it out and get a better look." He motioned for Tamar and Elisha to stand back. "Watch out everyone, this could be a priceless artifact, and we don't want it disintegrating into pieces."

Elisha's father gently tugged at the slab's edges, but they seemed embedded with time into the stone wall. Each time he tried pushing and pulling just a little bit harder, but nothing happened. Getting frustrated, his father complained loudly, "There's not enough light in here, I can't see a thing I'm doing."

Elisha was thinking that even if there were more light, his father wasn't going to be able to do it. He was far from being the strong, muscular type; the roughest surface he'd ever touched was his own laptop or ancient rare books.

After several gentle attempts, his father gave up the cautious method. He was already red in the face, gritting his teeth, and pushing his foot full force against the new family treasure. With a final heave, he gave up. And to everyone's utter disappointment, he announced, "This thing is stuck solid!! We'll have to get the workers to deal with it first thing tomorrow morning." He tried one more, full force, foot extraction, then added, "and they're probably going to charge an arm and leg to do it, too."

Elisha couldn't pull himself away that easily, despite being pushed out of a room for the third time in one day. There was something about that shiny slab, or whatever it was in the wall, and he was drawn to it.

Dr. Brody couldn't help fighting off a large degree of suspicion as he observed his final appointment of the day. There was no doubt that the young man was bright. He had the credentials, too, which was highly unusual for his young age. In fact, Dr. Brody had just finished reading a front page article from the day's newspaper which had been written by the young journalist, but probably, above all, what was most striking to the observing eye was his appearance. He looked like a top model that had just walked off a billboard selling luxury penthouses to the rich and famous. Dr. Brody glanced down at the file. He was only 22!!! Now that was hard to believe. Actually, it was incredulous. The young man radiated enough charisma and self-assurance to fill a stadium, which is probably what made him look much older. But, still . . . there was something *off* . . . and that was what Dr. Brody's profession was best at spotting.

"Are you going to take my case or not?" Jonathan Marks asked coolly and to the point.

Dr. Brody pretended to study the file. He realized that he only had seconds to make a decision and it wasn't an easy one. The prospective patient was seeking hypnotherapy, a series of hypnosis sessions to help him regain his memory. That would have been fine for any sort of regular trauma case that Dr. Brody was used to dealing with, but in this case, the patient claimed that his memory had been wiped out by a high school principal and a teacher four years earlier. That would also explain why Dr. Brody definitely remembered reading some scathing articles written by Jonathan Marks bashing some sort of private school in Jerusalem, but for the life of him, he couldn't remember the name of it. All of that, of course, seemed highly improbable. More than likely, the patient needed a good therapist, and he would be happy to refer him. IF it actually *had* happened, it would be uncomfortably scandalous. Dr. Brody wasn't particularly interested in either scenario, but in any case, he calmly asked, "Why now, Jonathan?"

Jonathan rattled off, "My response is handwritten on your form labeled 'number six, question 24' on the seventh line."

Dr. Brody shuffled the papers, while making a mental note to add to the file that the patient was also arrogant and had a photographic memory. He scanned the sheet, and indeed, on the seventh line, the patient had written that he had only realized the situation two months ago, after he had started getting flashbacks.

Jonathan was studying Dr. Brody's every reaction. He was expecting the doctor to ask him why he had waited two months, but he didn't bother. *Good.* Jonathan didn't want to have to think up some ridiculous excuse as to why he had prolonged seeking professional treatment until the New Moon of Tammuz.

Dr. Brody shut the file. Well, he didn't *like* the case, but it was intriguing nonetheless. He certainly never had a patient before with a photographic memory who had *lost* his memory. It would make an excellent article for the *Therapy and Hypnotherapy Journal*, and he hadn't submitted anything in quite a while.

"OK, Jonathan. We'll get right to work. Please make a series of appointments with my secretary, Keren," Dr. Brody said, while hitting the intercom button. "Keren, please schedule a series of ten consecutive sessions for Mr. Marks."

"I'm not going to call you again," was the loud threat Elisha's father used to coax him to the dinner table. Elisha begrudgingly showed up even though he didn't like non-family members eating with them. Even with his door closed, he had heard Gila's non-stop, high-pitched, baby voice that she always used to entertain Shira, but that was much better than having to look at her matching 'funny bunny' faces. It seemed that she even grated on Saba Gabriel's nerves because he definitely had earplugs in his ears, something which he never did when it was just the family. It was also Sunday night which meant Robert was over for dinner, if you could call it that. He was one of Elisha's mother's most 'special' students, meaning he was autistic and blind, so he was just standing around bumping himself into the table while randomly helping himself to food, some of which made it into his mouth.

That left Elisha as the only under-aged person required to sit in their seat throughout the meal, and it took all of his own self-control to stay in it. No one bothered asking him the usual 'how was school today?' because his father wanted to keep it a secret from Saba Gabriel, so Elisha didn't even get the chance to perform his re-enactment of the day's 'big event' which was now running in a constant re-play loop in his head. He practically bolted out of his chair when his mother finally got up, but she gestured for him to stay put, and then came back with a big cheese cake dripping with blueberry topping. She set it down on the table right in front of Saba Gabriel, and said indulgingly,

"Your favorite . . . to celebrate the New Moon."

Her smile was wide, but when Saba Gabriel didn't

react, it turned into concern until she quickly remembered, "Oh. I *forgot*. Those were only to block out the construction noise," and she quickly removed the two orange ear plugs hiding just behind his long white beard and repeated herself.

Saba Gabriel gazed at her lovingly, "But my dear child, the New Moon is supposed to be a holiday for women, and here you worked so hard."

Tamar Davidson was happy to report, "No, no, I bought it."

Now Saba Gabriel's whole face was beaming. He lowered his head in a small bow in Robert's direction and then slowly looked at everyone at the table, shining his inner radiance. They knew the look. It meant that they needed to leave some quiet space amid their usual chatting to let him say something, but it still irked Elisha that Robert and Shira were allowed to continue making a chorus of clunking noises.

When Saba Gabriel did speak, his voice trembled slightly. "I want you all to know that this is truly the best Tammuz of my life."

They all waited respectfully.

"This Tammuz marks the month that Elisha will be initiated into the Chambers Program!" His voice became infused with enthusiasm, "And I want to celebrate. I would like *all* of us to celebrate this monumental milestone."

Elisha looked away. He knew he wasn't supposed to handle this one.

Jessie Davidson did. But, he had no idea that his wife had already broken the bad news earlier in the afternoon, so he decided that glossing over it would be the best approach. He rose to the occasion by quickly mumbling,

"Well, not necessarily. There have been some last minute scheduling complications."

Saba Gabriel disregarded the information, "I assure you there aren't any, and Elisha will commence his initiation on the 17th. It will be one long unbroken chain."

Elisha brightened and asked, "Really?"

His father kicked him gently under the table.

"Absolutely. In fact, I received first-hand information from your school today, which is why I know without a shadow of a doubt that everything is going according to schedule for you."

Jessie Davidson was already eating the cheesecake and thinking *whatever you say*. Tamar Davidson just felt worried. *He's losing it. He's totally losing it*. But she still managed to guide Robert's hand away before he stuck it into the middle of the cake. Elisha didn't want to get kicked again, so he didn't ask *what information*?

Saba Gabriel held out his hands in Elisha's direction. Elisha walked over to him. He knew the Chamber initiation was a big deal for his great-grandfather, and he didn't want to disappoint him either. The elderly man hugged him and then placed his hands on top of Elisha's head and closed his eyes. Elisha waited expectantly for the monumental blessing, but instead Saba Gabriel fell instantly to sleep. Tamar Davidson sighed to herself, *really losing it*.

Elisha carefully and gently disengaged himself with his mother's approval. He then generously left Gila his dessert and slipped right back into the bathroom crevice.

He needed his own turn at dislodging the immense object. He stretched out his arms as far as he possibly could. His entire *almost*-11 year old body span was barely half the width of the gigantic stone, and even then, he only managed to get a grip on one side, which turned out to be a really bad idea. The massive stone just came right off the wall in an instant, without even making the slightest sound. It was extremely thick, and his fingers couldn't even hold onto the edges. In that split second, Elisha was sure that the oversized slab was going to come crashing to pieces all over his small body, but instead, it felt weightless, just like air in his hands. He gently set it on the floor. *OK, now explain that one!* He stood for a moment thinking it out and decided, *nah, Dad will definitely think he loosened it and it came down by itself.* Elisha's curiosity was now unbearable. He was desperate to move the mirrory-looking stone out of the crevice and to check and see if there was some kind of hidden passageway behind it, but he was sure the noise would attract everyone's attention. Instead, there was a different loud noise that caught his attention. It was a loud, incessant knock on their front door.

There was no 'hello', 'good evening', or 'sorry to interrupt your dessert', just an irate, "Don't you people know that there are laws prohibiting construction after 7:00pm?"

Elisha couldn't hear his father's response, but he clearly heard Mr. Magil, their next-door neighbor, getting even madder.

"*Really, now?* So, then *where* exactly are the sounds of a wild elephant crashing into our kitchen wall coming from??"

Elisha held his breath as he quietly tiptoed away from the 'crime' scene.

CHAPTER 2

Grandfathers, Grandmothers, & Avarshinas

Early the next morning, Elisha was shocked to see that the construction workers had beaten him to the bathroom. He was even more amazed to see three of the workers, including Dror, struggling to move the mirror slab under his father's orders and his mother's over-the-shoulder instructions. *But it can't be*, he thought to himself. It was off last night. Should he tell them all to stand back and he'd take care of it? Just as he was deliberating with himself, his mother caught sight of him.

"Elisha, it's late." She looked at her watch. "It's *very* late! Come on, finish getting dressed or you'll be late to school."

"SCHOOL!?" Elisha was stunned. "What's the point in going back *there* today? It's not like we're going to learn anything after what *happened* yesterday!" he re-marked bitterly.

"Don't even start," his father said sternly, which put a dead-end to it right there and then.

Elisha backed out of the bathroom and reluctantly headed towards the kitchen to pack his lunch. Poor Shira was put out of harm's way and was crying in her high chair, getting close to tantrum stage. Elisha picked up some toys for her and put them on the tray, but that made her cry even louder. *How could anyone go to school at a time like this???* He felt desperate, but playing sick wouldn't work at this point, so he resigned himself to being trapped. He grabbed his bag and quickly went, as usual, into Saba Gabriel's room to say goodbye.

The old man brightened the minute Elisha entered and slowly raised himself in bed. "Good, I've got you alone," he said with a smile. "Now tell me, Elisha my boy, what news can you bring me from the outside world?"

Elisha loved that opening line and never grew tired of hearing it. Saba Gabriel said it looking straight into his eyes. Their eyes did match. Elisha knew they did, except that on Saba Gabriel they looked *entirely* different. They were set deeply in his gentle, age-lined face and held the wisdom of having celebrated his 90th birthday last month. They were also framed with a snow white beard that fell way below his waist. Elisha figured the beard was probably close to celebrating 70. He could have easily told him the *whole* story about Professor Bezalel. Why did it have to be off limits? He hesitated and looked at one of his great-grandfather's favorite paintings on the wall. It was a massive black letter aleph set against a sky-blue background. There was something special about it that could make you stare at it for hours. He knew that Saba Gabriel was getting weaker. His parents kept whispering about it. Elisha had to admit it was true. Except for supper, he barely left his room. Everyone in the family was taking turns bringing him his breakfast and lunch for nearly a month already. Saba Gabriel was also a very patient man, so it was strange when he was the first to break the silence.

"Elisha. Your teacher was once *my* student, and a very prized one at that," he sighed sympathetically, and then strangely added, "it's the dark moon that has shadowed his vision."

Elisha was now on safe ground to spill it all. But he was also slightly confused because Saba Gabriel's last remark made it sound like his parents had served up a different version of the story, because he didn't remember anyone saying that Professor Bezalel had also become blind. Just then, his mother and her uncanny sixth sense abruptly intruded into the room with a serious whisk of wind, a breakfast tray, and a quick consultation of her watch.

"Here you are! You're going to be late. Get going," she commanded, while positioning her cheek for a good-bye kiss, even though Elisha wasn't in the mood now to give her one. He headed toward the door feeling a tinge of jealousy and a whole lot of frustration as he saw his mother settling down on the comfy bed and holding Saba's hand. But he wasn't going to be completely left out, even if he was being forcefully sent off to school.

"Mom, what about the mirror stone?"

"I'm calling an antiquities dealer today to get it appraised," but with irritation she added, "if only those workers could just get it off the wall".

"But you're not going to do anything with it before I come home, right?" Elisha was surprised to hear his own voice. It sounded like he was desperately pleading, "*Right*??"

But the only response he got was a kindly smile and her eyes motioning to the door again.

It was Saba Gabriel that answered, "I wouldn't dream of it."

That day at school, Elisha wondered how it was that parents could get their priorities so messed up. Wasn't it ridiculously obvious that it was much more important for him to stay home than to be a caged animal in this so-called classroom? And he had undergone a trauma, although his guilty conscience still hadn't told them why. There was only a week and half left of school, and it wasn't like anyone cared.

When Elisha entered his classroom his worst fears were confirmed. Mrs. Epstein had been brought in as a substitute teacher. She must have been well over 100 years old, with a short puffy wig that looked like a bird's nest and thick-as-a-fishbowl glasses that gave her eyes triple magnification. The real problem was that she was the kind of old lady that no one dared to start up with because she claimed to have known everyone's great-grandparents personally, and had seen the birth of most of their grand-parents, *and* had been their teacher too. And for some unexplainable reason, everyone felt they had to live up to her expectations of their having come from such 'fine families' and had to preserve their family's honor in her presence. That, or she'd rat on them to their grandparents and they'd never get a decent birthday present for the rest of their lives.

Today, however, she wanted everyone to sit in alpha-betical order to make it easier for her to remember their family names, as if this was worth the effort for the few

whole days left of school. While Mrs. Epstein didn't realize it, this was also *no* simple request. Professor Bezalel
always had strictly assigned seating by lineage. Priests,
Levites, and Israelites were grouped separately and each
had a different section of the room. It seemed unthinkable
to sit out of place. The Kohanim or priestly elite were on
the far right with the Levites next to them, and as they
were few in number, they barely took up two rows. The
rest of 'Israel', which included Elisha, sat in the middle
and to the left. Not that they were without distinction.
Everyone knew that the members of the House of David
were 'regular' Israelites, and it was the Davidic dynasty
that were the kings and built the Temple. This was, of
course, all totally lost on Mrs. Epstein, who was not happy repeating herself three times to the many descendents
of all the 'fine families' before anyone dared to move.
Elisha *knew* he shouldn't have come to school today. He
was still haunted about his 'involvement' in Professor
Bezalel's accident, and a part of him was just waiting for
two police officers to enter the classroom and arrest him,
with his fine lineage, as a fugitive assassin.

Mrs. Epstein, especially, was going to be torture,
because whenever she was a substitute there was *only* one
thing she taught and that was the 'art of penmanship',
a subject which she had surely made up because it was
not, to the best of anyone's knowledge, on any school
curriculum anywhere else in the country. And that only
added insult to injury, because in Professor Bezalel's class
students were *only* allowed to write in ancient paleo-He-
brew, a very cryptic hieroglyphic-looking alphabet that
none of their other teachers had ever bothered to learn
or decipher. There was actually only one very interesting
thing about Mrs. Epstein, and that was the small blue

number tattoo on her arm.

It took Elisha a second to shake off his daydreaming and see that the wrinkly tattooed arm was coming towards him and picking up his 'art'. The strong smell of mint and mothballs practically choked him, and when he looked up, it was straight into Mrs. Epstein's mega-magnified eyes. She flattened his paper and held it two inches from her face, then pursed her lips. She seemed very upset.

"Zhis iz atrrocious. Zimply atrrocious!!" She raised his paper in the air and announced, "Zhis iz exactly vhat happenz vhen you only know to uze computerz." She turned her attention back to Elisha and asked, "Do your parentz know about zhis?"

Elisha didn't know what to say. He hadn't really concentrated on his 'artwork', and as he looked at his paper, he realized that he had just automatically used the ancient Hebrew alphabet.

Mrs. Epstein quietly waddled back over to her desk in her orthopedic shoes and sat down with a loud thud. She took out a perfectly-pressed piece of pink writing paper, and with perfect penmanship started writing a letter which she read out loud at the same time for the class's benefit. "Dear Mr. and Mrz...," she coughed waiting for the name.

Elisha sighed and offered, "Davidson."

"I vaz deeply troubled to dizcover today zhat your young son, namely ...," again a cough.

"Elisha."

At this point, Elisha could tell that most of the class were practically killing themselves not to break out in hysterical laughter.

"Zufferz from a zevere motor skillz dizability."

That was it. Avshalom dropped to the floor in a fit.

Mrs. Epstein shifted her attention to the class. "Vhat? You tink I didn't know zhat fancy new name for being *chutzpadik*?" She rattled off in a sing-songy voice, "I know all of zhem. Zhis one haz ADD, zhen anozher vone comez up vit ADHD. Ve know all about it," she said with a wave of disgust. Pleased with her salient display of state-of-the-art pedagogic skills, she returned to her letter. "It painz me to be zhe one to have to deliver zhis discomforting newz, but he vill require immediate professional attention."

Even Josh was choking.

She raised her voice slightly and said, "I recommend zuzpending him from schule until zhis abnormality iz remedied, but I have made it a policy to alvayz give a varning first."

That statement had an amazing effect, and everyone quickly became straight-faced.

"Signed, Mrz. Esther Epstein."

The bell rang for the break, but Elisha had to remain seated and watch Mrs. Epstein neatly fold the letter, place it in a matching envelope, and lick it closed. She handed it to him with a satisfied look that the world was now one step closer to being a better place, and then asked, "Are you zhe son of Jessie Davidzon, Chief Librarian of zhe Hebrew Literature Archivez Institute?"

Elisha nodded reluctantly.

Mrs. Epstein sighed loudly, "Zhat vould make you zhe illustrious Gabriel Solomon'z great grandzon, vouldn't it?" She sighed louder, and when she breathed out, it was one big wheeze, "Vhat a shame zhat zhe apple has fallen so far from zhe tree."

Elisha shoved the horrid pink thing into his knapsack, fantasizing how he'd burn it into a pile of black ashes at the first available opportunity, but as he sat down, Mrs. Epstein wasn't through with him.

"Ah, ah, ah. You are going to stand *outzide* of zhe classroom as punishment for a full half hour, *and* you're going to hold zhe letter I gave you and tink about itz contentz, and *only* vhen you feel trrrue remorse can you come back into zeh classroom and join zeh fun."

Torture. That was all he could think about coming to school today, that and a growing resentment towards his parents for having had the bad judgment to have sent him here in the first place.

Principal Oholiov had missed seeing the mark of the Avarshina in the classroom. He actually hadn't looked for it, and it was also quite possible, that even if it had stared him in the face, he wouldn't have noticed it, but it was there. It was also the only reason why Professor Bezalel had survived that ominous day in the classroom.

Now the Avarshina wasn't just leaving its mark, it had come back. It watched silently from its embedded spot. It had wanted to touch the unique child, but now it was gone. It had wanted to see the *Shamir*, but it wasn't there. It closed its bejeweled eyes that were almost too old to see with anymore. It didn't matter; it didn't need to see. It had known every single classroom here intimately. Each one had been its nest. It had risen from the ashes here many a time. The school had what it needed most. It's what empowered it to be an Avarshina to begin with. It had lost count of its nests. It had lost count of the times it had ignited into flames, burned into ashes, and then lived again.

It had always curiously wondered why Mrs. Epstein didn't even know that it existed, especially since it was her father that had given it its new life. She was almost touching it, and yet she didn't see. Professor Bezalel *would* see the Avarshina, and he would understand. The Avarshina instinctively knew that it could only give its gift to Professor Bezalel. It sometimes thought it was the only reason why it had come to this place. Professor Bezalel would need it most. He would need it soon, but he hadn't asked for it, and now he was as good as ashes, and the Avarshina was very tired of being reborn.

As Elisha waited outside of his classroom, he actually thought it was more of a reward than a punishment, but that was until Principal Oholiov came down the hallway, and then Elisha wished he could have vanished into thin air.

Principal Oholiov noticed the Davidson kid the minute he had left his office. As he got closer, he also caught sight of the pink envelope. He stopped and coughed to clear his throat. The *last* thing he needed with all the recent public scrutiny and bad press was to get another complaint from an upset parent, and his dear Great-aunt Esther had a high batting average. The Davidson kid was also dangerous ground, because his mother was a teacher—Special Ed—autistic kids—which meant she would probably see Great-aunt Esther's note as tantamount to child abuse. He would *never* have brought her in, if it wasn't for all the last minute events with Daniel. He put on one of his less threatening smiles and said, "Davidson, I see you've managed to upset Mrs. Epstein?"

Elisha nervously shifted his position rather than responding.

"Well, what crime is it this time?" Principal Oholiov prompted again.

Elisha sheepishly and dutifully answered, "Um, I, ah, by accident used Professor Bezalel's script instead of regular and . . . ."

Principal Oholiov stopped him. "Good job, that's what you should be doing in Professor Bezalel's classroom."

Elisha was surprised, but it turned into shock when Principal Oholiov took the pink envelope out of his hands and said, "I'm sure this isn't necessary." Then he walked off with it, just like that, but as Elisha watched him head back to his office, he saw a police officer entering the school building just as Mrs. Epstein opened up the classroom door to call him back inside. Elisha was happy to take cover back in the safety of his classroom, but Mrs. Epstein was horrified to see that the note was missing.

"Vhere iz your note young man?" she demanded in a shrill and angry voice.

Elisha answered with a little too much smug satisfaction, "Principal Oholiov took it from me."

Mrs. Epstein's whole body seemed to turn red and blotchy.

Elisha didn't like the looks of her and suddenly felt a rising apprehension. What if Mrs. Epstein had a heart attack or something? Everyone knew that teachers were dropping like flies in their classroom, but his anxiety disappeared the minute Mrs. Epstein over-dramatically clutched at her desk with a look of steely determination.

She lowered her blotchy face and stared squarely through her magnifying glasses at the whole class. She motioned Elisha to sit down immediately, and once she was satisfied that she had everyone's complete attention, she folded her hands and waited. Elisha was already wishing she would speak.

She opened her mouth, closed it, and then in a strong whisper, she said, "You are playing vit fire in zhis very classroom! And little chilldren, *ezpecially* little chillldren should not be playing vit fire!!" She looked in both directions as if to make sure that the coast was clear, and then lowered her voice even more. "Don't you tink zhat I don't know vhat goez on in here! You tink I vas born yesterday? Zhat I don't know zhat zhey teach you . . . ," she hesitated and whispered, "*Kabbalah?*" Again, she secured her field of vision as if checking for enemy spies, "You tink I didn't recognize zhat *meshuganah* penmanship of zhe illustrious Gabriel Solomon'z great grandzon?? Now, you lizzen to Mrz. Epstein, and I'll really teach you sumtink." She straightened her suit, and in a scolding voice she said, "I know *all* about vhat you are doing. You tink you are vhat? Vizzardz? Zhat you have vite magic! You tink you can fight zhe dark side!!! Vell, Vell, Vell, bubbe-meisiz. You know nuttink! And I should know. I vaz in Auschwitz!" She let that one ring out and resonate. "Let me tell you sumtink else. My own fazher, my very own fazher, *may his zoul rest in peace*, who vaz alzo zhe very same great-grandfazher of your own principal, vell *he* vaz zhe *greatest* Kabbalist in all of Europe!" Her voice rose to a loud crescendo. "Do you hear me? And vhat do you tink zhe Nazi demonz, *zheir namez should be blotted out for eternity*, did to him? Now you tell me sumtink else. Vaz zhere a greater Kabbalist zhan zhe Sage Akiva from zhe Tahlmuhd? And vhat did ze Romanz, *zheir namez should be blotted out for eternity*, do to him?? I tell you vhat! Zhey ver bot torrtured to DET!!"

Mrs. Epstein adjusted her triple magnification glasses and scanned the classroom to make sure that her speech had the desired effect. Seemingly satisfied, she licked her parched lips, shifted in her seat, wrinkled her mouth into something that was supposed to be a smile, and tried to regain her grandmotherly composure.

"Zilly vizzardz are only in story bookz, and apparently your parentz and teacherz let you read too many of zhem."

The whole class was exchanging glances. For all of her 100 old-lady years, Mrs. Epstein was terrifying. She was also misinformed. They never practiced *Kabbalah* in their classroom. It was only taught in the Chambers, and even there, everyone had heard that it was only a tiny, small part of the program.

"Now vee vill continue do to sumtink trrruly vortvile, and even it vill be like a fun game for you."

No one could guess what that would be.

"Vee are all going to write a get-vell card for your poor, sick, and very mizguided teacher, *may he have a speedy recovery*, in our best penmanship." She smiled again, and struggling against gravitational pull, she got up, smoothed her three-piece navy blue polyester suit, and started to slowly lick her finger to pass everyone precisely *one* piece of precious pink stationary. "And I vant long letterz, or you can write a long poem if you vant, cauze he haz a lot of time to read zhem."

Elisha stared blankly at the fine, pink, unlined abyss. He didn't want to write on anything that Mrs. Epstein had just licked. But, he begrudgingly started composing in his mind, *Dear Professor Bezalel, you were looking at me before you crushed your head*. It occurred to him that he could easily turn this into a poem because lots of things rhymed with head, but everyone else looked too busy writing already, so he took the straight approach and his get-well letter sounded boring and totally uninteresting. He wouldn't have been surprised if poor Professor Bezalel was going to get 30 pink pieces of paper that would give him more amnesia. No one dared to speak during the 'game', and everyone made sure that his penmanship was perfect. By the last hour of school, Elisha had counted down from sixty nearly sixty times, waiting for the bell to ring. Even before its first full zing, the entire class was already shooting off like high strung arrows and quickly abandoning their 'art'. Josh was running alongside Elisha.

"Hey! Where are you running to?" he panted. "Remember, you're a striker today at Avi's."

Elisha had entirely forgotten. His only focus after surviving Mrs. Epstein was to get home to the mirror stone. "Oh wow, I can't today."

"What? Are you kidding? You HAVE to, come on."

Suddenly, Elisha found Josh very annoying. There were some things that you didn't share even with your best friends. He was surprised to hear the tone of his own voice when he broke off, "I told you. No. Now will you just leave me alone!"

Josh's face registered complete hurt, but Elisha, well, he just didn't have time to deal with it, not today.

"I always like to start from the beginning," was how Dr. Brody opened his first session with Jonathan Marks.

"But, I don't," answered Jonathan a little bit too sharply, so he immediately added in a softer tone, "because Dr. Brody, it's highly unnecessary in my case. In a nutshell, I was born, had a great childhood, did phenomenally well in school, I'm perfectly normal, and life is just fine. So now that the introductions are over, can we just start with filling in the blanks from four years ago?"

He wasn't a very pleasant character, thought Dr. Brody, but he knew he couldn't force a patient that wasn't ready yet to express himself, so he calmly followed along. "Okay, that's also a good place to start. Why don't you tell me, Jonathan, why you believe that you've lost some of your memory?"

"I don't *believe*, I know."

That may be the case in your own mind, thought Dr. Brody, and he smiled inwardly because he was now observing for the first time signs of anxiety in the patient's usually cool composure. Jonathan seemed to be flustered, trying to concentrate on something that his quick mind couldn't crack. Dr. Brody coaxed him on. "What was the name of the high school you attended at the time?"

"If you can call it a high school," Jonathan added with a degree of disgust. "It's called the North Temple Mount Academy," but then he reclined in his chair, crossed his legs, and put on an air of waxing poetic with a sarcastic tone. "Yes, it's an ancient institution, located in the picturesque Old City of Jerusalem, eternal capital of King David, center of the world. *If I forget thee O' Jerusalem, let my right hand forget its skill . . . .*"

"Did you have an unpleasant experience there?" asked Dr. Brody.

"*Obviously*, if I'm here and told you why I need you."

Dr. Brody was used to patients and their defense mechanisms at work. He just waited in silence for more to emerge and it did.

"It's a school for freaks," Jonathan corrected himself, "an exclusive private school for freaks. The principal is Ezra Oholiov, but it's really run by Professor Daniel Bezalel. Ever hear of him?"

"No, I haven't," answered Dr. Brody in all honesty.

"Well Google him and get impressed," Jonathan said, as he swiftly rattled off Professor Bezalel's bio. "He was *born* Paul Montgomery the Third, Church of England, but he 'switched teams' and became Daniel Bezalel just in time for his bar mitzvah, and then moved to Jerusalem. Today, he has more degrees and titles than the whole Jewish Quarter put together: Professor, Doctor—as in *eight* PhDs, Rabbi, Director of this Temple institute he founded, and the list goes on and on. And get this, he's even Sir, as in knighted by the Queen of England herself!"

Dr. Brody had to admit it was an impressive bio, but it was the seething hatred in Jonathan's voice that was even more remarkable. He made a note of that, too, and continued with his carefully phrased questioning. "What makes them 'freaks' in your opinion?"

Jonathan stared straight into Dr. Brody's eyes and said, "It's actually that they're mentally unstable, and in their insanity, they want to brainwash everyone to be like them."

"And what does it mean to be *like* them?"

Jonathan hesitated. He had to be careful at this point, because if his suspicions were correct, then the outlandish truth would even ruin his own credibility at this early stage. He decided he'd give Dr. Brody a small part of the truth, at least the tip of the iceberg, which he could probably digest. "Practicing Kabbalah masters."

That didn't sound so bad to Dr. Brody. Kabbalah was highly popular these days. It was sort of trendy and 'in'. Wasn't it just another one of those ancient pathways to attain personal fulfillment? He personally didn't know the first thing about it, but every other week there was some new Hollywood celebrity endorsing it. He even remembered seeing an infomercial for it. That couldn't have been so bad. *No.* He would need to be patient to find out what was really underlying it all.

Jonathan was still staring at him, and he hadn't even blinked.

"Dr. Brody, I guarantee you that you have *no* idea what a *real* practicing Kabbalah master is. What you're thinking about celebs and infomercials, well, that's a joke."

Dr. Brody shifted uneasily in his chair. Jonathan Marks was starting to give him an unsettling feeling.

Elisha was out of breath when he reached home, but this time it was from excitement rather than fear, and he could feel his face afire from the blistering sun. Once again he accidentally slammed the front door with his hasty entrance and no one yelled out. Elisha went straight to the bathroom and could see why. The antiquities appraiser must have just gotten there. Shira was in his mother's arms sucking very noisily on an empty bottle, and the minute his mother spotted him, she quickly passed Shira into his arms.

"Oh good, you're here, please take Shira out so Mr. Pollock can work."

Elisha wasn't going anywhere. He wanted to watch Mr. Pollock 'at work'.

The stone was still stuck in the wall, and it was clear that Mr. Pollock didn't want to risk getting even one speck of dust on any part of his expensive suit while making the appraisal. He inched towards the wall carefully, constantly checking to see that he had cleared the broken-down cinder blocks on both sides. It seemed to Elisha that his whole face was pinched-in with annoyance.

The family practically held their breath while Mr. Pollock adjusted his glasses once, twice, and then a third time, before he quickly and abruptly announced:

"Mr. and Mrs. Davidson, you should be more prudent next time. It's completely obvious that this object is an entirely worthless heap of refraction, and you've taken up too much of my valuable time on this nonsense."

Elisha felt his entire body relax.

The appraiser promptly left the dirty construction site, wearing an expression that said he was now in a desperate need of a bath. He brushed off both arms of his suit and firmly said, "Good day!"

Elisha couldn't help smirking to himself, but his parents looked utterly disappointed. As far as Elisha was concerned, life was looking good again. He didn't have a pink note to 'share', the Holocaust was safely over at least a hundred years ago, and he could still make it in time for the game.

That's if you could call it a game. It was more like Elisha and nine other kids bumping into each other, all of them insanely stubborn in their denial that it was just too scorching hot out to play. They were all missing every other move in their worst game ever.

Josh was the only one who had the good sense to end it. He raised both his hands up and then leaned them on his knees, panting, and said, "Forget it guys, we're all going to *die* in this heat. I'm out."

No one needed convincing.

Elisha flopped down on the scraggly grass as Avi dropped the soccer ball and toppled down right next to him.

"We're all going to collapse like you know who," he gasped.

A figure cast a shadow on both of their faces. It was Joseph, a tall and serious boy. Whether he heard Avi or not, he joined in, "He's going to need surgery, you know. My Dad said so."

Elisha thought Joseph would know since his father was Chief Surgeon at Mt. Scopus. Elisha tried being calm and conversational. "For the amnesia?" he asked.

Joseph choked on his water and laughed, "No, you idiot, for his gastro disease."

Elisha wasn't offended. In his fear of self-preservation, it seemed like a brilliant cover to be labeled stupid.

It was Gadi that dramatically changed the subject.

"I think I can find the Vault."

That immediately earned him everyone's attention, but Joseph was in his usual skeptical form. "No, you can't. No one can, and you don't even know any initiates."

Gadi smiled. "Oh yes, I do. My sister Rachel was there last year and all it will take is a little brotherly torture to get the information." He looked around. "Who's in?"

Joseph scoffed. "If it was that easy, don't you think

I'd know by now? I've got four of my own moronic sisters at home and *none* of them ever talked."

"That's because you don't know how to be convincing," Gadi said, with a mean streak in his eyes.

Avshalom came to Gadi's aid and said confidently, "I can help."

Elisha looked at his sneakers and thought, *I am out of here.*

Avshalom was suddenly hovering over his body and taunting, "Elisha will be coming too."

Elisha gave him the worst scowled expression he could muster, but Avshalom just stared at him, and stared at him, and then stared at him some more, and pretended to fall down. Elisha *got* the blackmail message. He froze momentarily, feeling like his stomach had just free-fallen 20 storeys. He also couldn't think of a single thing to say, so he just stood up, shook off the dried grass that had collected on his shorts, and walked slowly out of the park. He didn't see Josh leaving in disgust after him, but he had heard the laughing reverberating in his head.

After turning the corner, Elisha hurried back home, trying to keep down the rising nausea in his stomach. When he got there, he went straight to the bathroom and threw up; his mother said it was dehydration. But she was also overwhelmed: No available babysitters, a houseful of construction workers on overtime, Dad working late, something about it being impossible to find a doctor to make a housecall for Saba, and ordering a pizza. Elisha reluctantly took the two-liter bottle of mineral water that was being forced into his hands and shut his bedroom door on all of it. He then proceeded to shut down his mind as well. He sat down comfortably determined to set a new record on Flightpilot. It took hours, but he even made level 12.

She had never been in the Foundation Vault, but she knew exactly where it was. The 'rest' of the class was always inside it.

British and Israeli archaeologists also knew. It was located under the Master Course of the Second Temple's foundations on Mount Moriah. They had proven its existence, but they couldn't accurately gauge its dimensions. All they knew was that there was a void—some kind of empty space—under the four massive Herodion stones that made up the Master Course. They realized that these stones served as some sort of counterforce to protect the vault, but since the Master Course itself was 118 feet wide, no one even thought of tampering with it, especially because one of the four stones was a whopping 44 feet wide and weighed over 600 tons! Certainly whatever was under there wasn't worth endangering the stability of the Western Wall, the *Kotel*. After all, it was all that was left of the Second Temple—one *last* remaining courtyard wall. And it *definitely* wasn't worth weakening the foundations of the Temple Mount itself—the very site of Solomon's Temple—*the* most sacred Jewish site for over 3,000 years. Even more precarious was the Dome of the Rock Mosque that had been constructed precisely on top of the Temple's ruins. Obviously, any tampering with the current Moslem holy site would be enough to set off World War III, so they left it at that. They knew for a fact that there was no way to access it, and each one of them would have staked his professional reputation and career on it. What they also didn't know was that there was no need to accurately gauge dimensions in the vault. There weren't any.

"Mrs. Bezalel," the nurse said firmly, "your husband *will* have to undergo surgery today," and she kindly reminded her with a singsong voice, "you *did* hear what the doctor said, didn't you?"

Rebecca was staring out the window, and sang back under her breath, "I'm not the one with the amnesia." She immediately stopped herself and buried her tired face in her hands. She wasn't even sure what was the matter. She had known from day one that Daniel was a sick man. The head injury wasn't the problem. None of this was new. She had even expected complications right after their wedding. But for some reason, having survived without incident for fifteen years, and after three kids, she had forgotten about this inevitable day, even though she was so sure that she had spent all those same years preparing for it. Well, here it was, and she wasn't prepared. And she already felt totally alone, because Daniel didn't have any idea who she was anyway.

So, that's how it would be. She composed herself and signed some more papers on the clipboard that was being shoved into her face. She didn't even give them the slightest review. When she looked up, Ezra was standing over her, and she was startled for a moment. She had been so dazed and drained that she hadn't even noticed him come in.

He offered her his hand. She took it. He was trying to be kind and supportive.

"There isn't a human being alive with more energy. It will take a lot more than one risky surgery to keep him down, and you know it."

She did know it, but she also knew what Ezra couldn't fathom, and that only made it worse. She was too exhausted to fight, and the thought of having a caring older brother by her side in the waiting room now was better than keeping him as an enemy. She nodded, and let his extended hand help pull her and her over-sized eighth-month stomach out of the low visitor's chair. One more month left to go. She had to be strong. Daniel had told her that this child was going to be very special. Well, he or she would be, if he or she would be born on the 9th of Av. Daniel knew everything. Once, that is.

Elisha was tossing and turning in his bed. Even six straight hours of Flightpilot hadn't managed to clean the disc in his brain, and he was going in and out of a restless, yet deep, sleep. Maybe the antiquities dealer was lying; anyone could tell that it was something valuable. He supposed his parents were upset because they probably could have used the money. But it was always Professor Bezalel's last, haunting stare that kept reappearing between every thought. He woke up. He realized it was high time to tell his parents about it, but the sudden sound of heavy dragging footsteps interrupted his thoughts. Elisha was surprised at how quickly he jumped out of bed. What time was it? A glance at his watch confirmed that it was 3:30 in the morning. He quietly started for his door in the dark and was met by a weird sight. It was Saba Gabriel on the way to Elisha's room. Elisha ran to his side.

"Saba, what's the matter? Can I get you something? Saba, you shouldn't be out of bed."

Saba Gabriel gently patted his hand. "No need to worry," he said, and with smiling eyes he added, "so are you going to help me move the stone into your room, or do you want me to do it myself?"

Elisha suddenly felt he was in a dreamy confusion, where the ridiculous was somehow making sense.

"No Saba, it's way too heavy for you. I'll take care of it. You go back into bed."

Elisha helped him move slowly back to his room as Saba gripped the doorpost.

"Alright. A good night's sleep would do me good now, but only if you promise me that you'll watch over it for us both."

Elisha went along with the strange charade and was quick to agree. When had Saba ever made him promise anything? He walked Saba slowly back in the direction of his room, one tiny step at a time, so slowly that between every one of those small steps you could fall asleep, and he really had not completely woken up to begin with. At one point, his great-grandfather had said something in a faint voice about 'news from the outside world'. All Elisha could concentrate on was getting Saba back into his bed, but did he really get around to it? The only thing he remembered was seeing his pillow again.

The room was roughly circular. The ceiling was low. The air was absolutely still. It was the perfect place to learn the difference between understanding and wisdom. There was a difference, a BIG difference. Understanding was what everyone did. They did it by using pictures and words with each other. They would show somebody a picture of something or explain something with words and then they would *understand*. Wisdom was something *else*. Wisdom was something you didn't use words for. She knew, because you could only see the point of infinity with wisdom; no one could explain it to you in words or take a picture of it and show it to you. It was the same with nothingness. You could only see nothingness with wisdom; no one could explain what nothingness looked like or take a picture of it and show it to you.

You could only have wisdom if you didn't fill your head with thoughts, because thoughts were things you understood. She liked wisdom better, because wisdom was a world without words. Most people liked to be in a world with words. She didn't. She didn't like how people would say words to her and show her pictures of things they wanted her to understand.

There was only one thing that connected the world with words and the world without words. It was the letters. But in the world without words, the letters were of course different, because they weren't used for words anymore.

If you didn't know wisdom, then you couldn't begin, because you could only see the Sephirot with wisdom, and you could only peek quickly. And they were always only for a flash and then they would disappear. If you tried to see them with understanding, your mind would be swallowed up with too many pictures that you could never *understand*, and then you could not even come back. She saw that people who were really good at *only* understanding things would lose all of their understanding if they had to look at pictures that they couldn't understand. That's what happened to two of the boys.

She knew. But they were fixed. They hadn't listened really well. They were told to run and return. They were told that if they stayed too long in wisdom they would end up being in big trouble. They were told that they had to always run, and then return back to the regular world of words and understanding. She never had a problem doing it. She would pretend that she was on a swing, and then she could swing back and forth from understanding to wisdom. Back and forth. Back and forth. But really it was forth, forth, forth, forth, back. Forth, forth, forth, forth, back. Because most of the time she had wisdom in her mind and not understanding.

Elisha's room was bright with the morning rays of a strong summer sun when the fuzziness of his deep sleep started wearing off, but the sight he woke up to didn't hold the expectations of a beautiful summer's day. Why was his mother crying on his bed, and why was she holding his hand?

"Elisha," she rasped, while wiping away tears.

He could see that her usually bright green eyes were dull, red, and puffy.

"I'm sorry," she said, and clasped his hand harder with her wet one.

What was it? Elisha was sure he did *not* want to know, but she continued in her hoarse voice.

"We had to take Saba Gabriel to the hospital last night."

Elisha couldn't believe it! He immediately thought that the mid-night walk around the house must have been too difficult for him. He was instantly wide awake and ready to get out of bed.

"But, but last night he was even walking around the house. I saw him, and he seemed so strong."

His mother gave him an even sadder look, and that really annoyed him because Elisha wasn't about to back off, and he quickly remembered the proof.

"Last night at 3:30! I even looked at my watch, and Saba was coming to my room."

His mother wasn't listening, and started caressing and straightening his hair. She hugged him, resting her head of the same color hair onto his own. She had a strained look of trying to be tender.

"Elisha, we took Saba to the hospital at 12:30 last night. You must have been dreaming."

"NO! I spoke to him!" Elisha's body was rigid as he started moving out of bed. "I'm coming with you right now," he said, but his mother's arms gently kept him in place.

"Saba Gabriel passed away just a few hours after we got him there."

That was more than enough. Elisha couldn't stand to hear any more of these outrageous words.

"NO! Mom, no! *YOU'RE WRONG*. I SAW him, I spoke to him."

His mother was entirely unfazed. She just continued speaking in her bereaved voice. "He just shut his eyes and went to sleep so peacefully. He was smiling," and then proudly she added, "he was 90 years old, he lived a full life."

If she was trying to console herself with her own words, it didn't work, because the tears were coming out of her eyes even faster.

Her words were slowly taking on the weight of real meaning, and just the thought of it hurt so much that Elisha couldn't even blink or swallow. Was it possible that that's the way things happened, just like that, without getting some kind of tiny warning first, a hint, a sign, anything at all? His mother's tears were proof that it was. He understood.

CHAPTER   3

The 36

There were crowds of people at the funeral and lots of boring and never-ending speeches, but Elisha didn't hear or see much. His eyes were foggy with tears that just stuck to the bottom of his long eyelashes and didn't drop off.

In the ancient Jerusalem tradition, his great-grandfather was wrapped in an all-white *tallit* and laid out on a long rectangular block of solid rock. Elisha couldn't stand seeing the shape; it couldn't be Saba Gabriel in there. A large group of men carried the shape outdoors while the relentless sun beat down on everyone's head and mind. As Elisha watched the shape disappear into the abyss of an oversized van, he said his last goodbyes inside himself.

It was strange to think how he had rushed home yesterday to see the stone, as if it was the only thing that mattered in the world. If he had only known, he would have rushed home to spend some last moments with Saba Gabriel. He had even traded that moment for Flightpilot. He'd never have the chance to say a real goodbye now, and a dry lump the size of a baseball lodged in his throat and stung his eyes. That was it for grandparents now too. His father's parents lived in Arizona, wherever that was, and he had only seen them twice in his life. He had never even met his mother's parents. They had died when she was just a little girl. It was only now, in the shadow of his first-hand experience with death, that Elisha thought that was weird, but he was sure his mother must have been too little to have understood anything, wasn't she? And of course it didn't seem to matter because they had Saba Gabriel instead. He was like her real father. But, now it would just be lonely them from now on. But of course, he couldn't avoid the thought that was foremost in his mind: the dream. It was now clearly obvious that's what it was, and yet he couldn't remember it as a dream, as much as he tried. He was sure it had happened, even though he had to admit that it had some fuzzy edges to it. Also, do promises matter if you make them in a dream?

The first actual hypnosis session was a bonafide success all around. After some convincing, Jonathan had agreed to allow Dr. Brody to start his hypnotic regression from the time of his first contact with Professor Bezalel and Principal Oholiov in his 'so-called' Chamber One program. He was only 11 years old at the time, but there was no doubt that the images were disturbing. Jonathan had described being in a subterranean vault deep under the Western Wall, and the lessons he had repeated were of such an advanced metaphysical nature that it was absolutely incomprehensible why children of such a young age were expected to even follow *any* of the concepts. They were way over Dr. Brody's own head, but even so, he strained to understand as Jonathan calmly repeated the ideas.

"The Sephirot manifest themselves in the physical world in water which is the pionic force, fire—the electromagnetic force, and air, the weak nucleus force. Earth is gravity. Everything is in the Tetragrammaton, the ineffable, four letter Name, the One Who Is, Was, and Will Be."

Dr. Brody honestly couldn't understand a word, and yet, it was clear that the 11-year old Jonathan was strangely recounting a mixture of theology and philosophy along with what seemed like university-level physics. After the session, Jonathan had corrected him and explained that it was, "all just theoretical Kabbalah mumbo-jumbo," but the satisfaction on Jonathan's face when Dr. Brody played back the session was apparent.

"I think I've got more than enough now to work with," Jonathan gloated. "They're twisted. They're actually brainwashing kids in an underground vault. This is more than sufficient evidence to warrant a full-blown investigation."

Dr. Brody hesitated. He knew all too well that many courts had banned hypnosis testimony and the authorities were highly skeptical. Not only that, but he hadn't had enough sessions to professionally establish whether or not Jonathan's case was simply one of FMS—False Memory Syndrome. He tried his best to dissuade Jonathan from jumping too far ahead and to at least give it a little more time.

It was only when Jonathan was taking the elevator down from the 21st floor that he started having second thoughts. The minute the doors closed, the luxurious mirrored and aluminum interior started jiggling like Jell-O on every side. It barely lasted five seconds, but Jonathan still lunged to grab hold of the side bar. He could see the reflection of his face sweating profusely. He could also clearly see that the young couple in the elevator not only hadn't experienced it, but they were looking at him like he was a psychopath and practically ran out of the elevator when it reached the ground floor. Jonathan was sure that he had just experienced some sort of bizarre side effect from the hypnosis, but for some unnamed reason, it also convinced him that he should wait a little longer before going to the police.

The *shivah*, the 'seven' days of mourning had started immediately. The house was a revolving door of visitors, with everyone saying the same thing. His great-grand-father had been one of the '36'. Elisha knew what they meant. He also knew it was the highest compliment any-one could give. He didn't know where the story had come from, but there were supposed to be 36 people walking around the planet that were guardians of the universe. Actually, they were *secret* guardians of the universe. It was a kind of hidden identity thing. There were only 36 in the whole world at any given time, only 36 in each generation. And without the 36, the universe would sim-ply self-destruct, because it was only on account of these 36 special people that it didn't blow up in the first place, but Elisha sadly understood that like everything else, even the 36 were replaceable.

All of the kids from Elisha's school had courteous-ly come too. No matter what, the conversation always uncomfortably led back to Professor Bezalel's amnesia, and to him needing a series of complicated surgeries, and how there wouldn't be any Chamber One summer camp this year. Josh wasn't angry anymore. Of course, now he thought he understood why Elisha had acted so meanly that day, and he was quite happy to help himself to the many refreshments that were set out on the tables for the visitors. Elisha thought everything was tasteless. His classmates also tactlessly told him how lucky he was to get out of the last week of school with Mrs. Epstein, as if this was a better fate.

All the mirrors in the house were covered over, as was the custom during the shivah, so Elisha respectfully resisted having a look at the biggest one. But he couldn't help feeling a deep childish envy as he watched Gila working around the clock to keep Shira out of the house. He was too old to go with her, and also too young for any of the visitors to share their stories with him. So, he was left mostly alone and yet always had to be on hand as 'Exhibit A': the great-grandson of the 'illustrious Gabriel Solomon'. As far as he could tell, there wasn't much involved. He wasn't even expected to smile back at anyone as they nodded, pointed or beamed in his direction.

But, it was strange for Elisha to see that he shared Saba Gabriel with so many people. He had known that Saba had been really important, but in the past five years that he had lived in their home, he kept to his room most of the time, with his books, and just the family. His parents had disapproved of visitors because of his bad health. Now, Elisha had never seen so many different kinds of people coming into his house. There were all sorts of government dignitaries and parliament members and a never ending trail of crying people of all ages, colors, and dress that needed to look at 'Exhibit A'.

It was on the last day of the shivah that the strangest visitor of them all showed up, and the minute he did, there was a tangible hush that came over the entire room. Elisha couldn't help thinking to himself that this squat-looking man was the spitting image of Doc from Snow White and the Seven Dwarfs. However, his parents seemed really honored at the presence of this man and were going out of their way to show it. It was clear to Elisha that the man didn't like the attention, and as he found a place to sit, Elisha noticed that he was looking intently at all the faces around the room, but then locked his gaze on Elisha. Now it was Elisha's turn to feel very uncomfortable, especially since the squat man got up and was now walking right towards 'Exhibit A'. Luckily, his father was quick to his feet and followed right behind the man, while gesturing in the strongest terms for Elisha to STAND UP. He did so immediately, just as the man asked ever so slowly, "So, you're the one, aren't you?"

Elisha couldn't explain why, but this man's eyes weren't acknowledging, beaming or just looking at him. He felt they were X-raying him, and his simple question hit him straight in his gut. Elisha didn't know what to say, and his guilt-laden heart fell to the floor. He was sure that Professor Bezalel's prosecutor had finally found him, and he held his breath wondering how to state his confession. Thankfully, his father rescued him.

"Yes, honorable Rav Kadosh, this is my eldest son, Elisha."

The Rav's expression showed that he knew that already.

"Elisha, this is the great Mekubal, Rav Yehuda Kadosh."

The Rav continued to stare straight at him, sizing him up. He seemed noticeably unimpressed. Elisha had no idea what to do with himself. He could feel himself turning red from head to toe. Rav Kadosh suddenly shut his eyes tight, and when he opened them he said, "Here's my card, young man. You'll know when you need it."

He handed Elisha a miniature book of *Tehillim*, King David's Psalms, that wasn't much bigger than his palm. Elisha turned all his attention to it, which was certainly better than facing Mekubal 'Doc' again. The cover had a colorful picture of the Choshen, the High Priest's breast-plate, which was a popular drawing on many miniature prayer books. Elisha wondered how this was a 'card', but he respectfully took it and managed to say, "Thank you." He was actually very relieved that the Rav's short shivah call was over and he was on his way out the door, but as Elisha continued to stare at the small cover of the 'card', he was seized again by panic, wondering if there was a connection. After all, before IT happened, Professor Bezalel was talking about the Choshen.

That night Elisha reviewed all the events of the past week very carefully in his mind. There was no doubt about it, finally at almost age 11, life was getting very complicated. A part of him logically knew that he had nothing to do with Professor Bezalel's accident, but then why was he too scared to confide in anyone about his secret guilt? He assured himself that it was probably because he knew it was ridiculous. He looked at the 'calling card' again. He would have to live with the wave of nagging nausea that the Mekubal's card had aroused in him, because he had already decided to take action tomorrow on something much more important. Whether Saba Gabriel's nighttime visit was real or a dream, the conversation had happened; he was sure of it, absolutely sure. Positive.

In Dr. Brody's professional opinion, *the* turning point took place during the third hypnosis session. He had no idea that for Jonathan Marks it was a turning point that came with extreme side effects.

Dr. Brody was making quick progress and had regressed Jonathan to the Third Chamber. He was thirteen years old, but now the theoretical 'mumbo-jumbo' had become practice. Dr. Brody was astounded to hear Jonathan being instructed in some sort of technique to alter his consciousness. He grabbed his notepad and listened intently as Jonathan recounted.

"We're in the subterranean vault now, and Professor Bezalel will instruct us on how to develop an inner sight to view the world."

Dr. Brody started scribbling frantically.

"The sphere of the intellect has the power and speed to travel through the spiritual realm, which is the realm of Pure Intellect. Today we will attain synesthesia, where sound is seen and colors are heard."

Dr. Brody was raising both his eyebrows when Jonathan suddenly shifted positions and said, "It is time to position ourselves."

Dr. Brody watched as Jonathan got up from the sofa and started to carefully move himself into a strange position. He was on the floor, lowering his head and aligning it between his knees.

"We must divest all of our thoughts and even our power of speech. We will oscillate between verbal consciousness and nonverbal consciousness. We will run and return. Professor Bezalel will now arrange the letters, and we will recite the permutations of the names."

Jonathan started a haunting chant that seemed to be made up of fragments of Hebrew letters and meaningless words. It went on for quite a while until he said, "Our visions will be like a reflection on a pool of water. I cannot allow even one thought into my mind or the water will ripple and the entire vision will be lost."

Jonathan was now singing rather than chanting the strange syllables and the melody was so eerie that Dr. Brody suddenly felt a terrible sense of complete disorientation, even in his own office. He quickly decided to end the session, and it was just as Jonathan had lifted up his head and said, "We are preparing to enter the first hall."

Dr. Brody didn't need any more convincing. He smiled at Jonathan and handed him the recording. He then helped him back onto the sofa.

"I think you're ready. That is, if you still want to bring in the police."

Jonathan didn't seem to react right away. He seemed dazed and confused. Dr. Brody buzzed Keren and asked her to bring in some water, which she delivered only too happily with her brightest smile. It occurred to Dr. Brody that *he* never got a glass of water with that much efficiency or decorum. He took the glass out of her hand and passed it on to Jonathan. In seconds, the full glass was accidentally knocked to the floor and a large darkened spot was forming on Dr. Brody's sea blue carpet. Jonathan didn't apologize, but Keren did it for him.

"No worries, it won't leave a stain."

Jonathan was rubbing his temples with his eyes closed. He was still trying to totally eradicate the disturbing vision he had seen in that glass of water.

Rebecca and Ezra didn't have to say a word to each other to know what they were both feeling. It was hope. They were really hoping that when Daniel woke up from this second surgery that he would be Daniel again. The doctors had told them that surgery could trigger a recovery from amnesia, but it certainly didn't work the first time around. So, now they were being cautiously hopeful, while the kids were being completely annoying, and Rebecca wished she had left them at home with a babysitter instead of having dragged them with her to the hospital. They were fidgety, bored, and started fighting with each other over nothing. When they found the electric button that raised the hospital bed, Rebecca started losing it.

Ezra also picked up on that cue, and in his role as favorite uncle, he asked, "Who wants to go and get a snack with me from that really fun machine downstairs?"

The amount of excited, "I do's," were triple the amount of kids, and they all happily trailed after him and out of the hospital room.

Rebecca leaned back in the chair and closed her eyes. She was silently willing him to come back, over and over again in her mind.

Barely five minutes had passed when the no-nonsense-ever head nurse made an entry with a stiff, "and how is our Professor Bezalel doing after his surgery?"

Rebecca didn't open her eyes. That nurse had always irked her, and he wasn't *our* Professor Bezalel, but she did offer, "He hasn't woken up yet."

"Well, yes, he has," said the nurse, while checking the IV drip attached to his arm.

Rebecca quickly looked to her side, but even before she did, she sensed it, and she was right. Daniel was just staring blankly at the ceiling. Their eyes met briefly and he even seemed bored to see her. He shut his eyes and went back to sleep. *No!* It still wasn't *him*, and she couldn't help herself and started crying.

If she hadn't been so preoccupied with her own misery, she would have noticed that he was silently mouthing something. It was inaudible, but also unmistakable. He was clearly mouthing the words, "I'm Paul. Paul Montgomery the Third."

The head nurse's response to Rebecca's lowered head was stern.

"Now really, is that any way to be thankful that your husband came out of his surgery with flying colors!" The nurse busied herself with more connections and digital hospital monitors, and then briskly walked out of the room.

Even with all the distractions of unwrapping candy bars, Ezra guessed the outcome of the operation the minute he came through the door. He couldn't hide his disappointment either, and he just flopped down in the other chair, holding two of the kids on his lap while using their backs to block his view.

It was a relief to wake up on the last day of the shivah to a house empty of visitors, but it also left a gaping hole of loneliness. Elisha knew that that hole wasn't going to disappear, and it was only his plan of action for the mirror stone that focused him enough to try and get back to his morning routine. That and the promise he had made in his 'dream' to his great-grandfather. He wasted no time. He went straight to the stone and easily dislodged it, then he moved it to the side.

To his utter disappointment, there was absolutely *nothing* behind it. No secret passageway, no revolving doors or cryptic messages. He even tried tapping the wall every few centimeters and foolishly chanted *Abracadabra*, but absolutely nothing happened. Deflated, Elisha went about the task of moving the stone into his room. Weird as it was, the massive slab was almost weightless, and he easily maneuvered it along, even though its height just barely cleared the doorpost of his bedroom.

Away from the dark, cramped construction 'cave', and in the bright sunlight of his room, Elisha could inspect the stone carefully for the first time. It had a dull, misty, light blue finish that didn't quite qualify it for the job of a mirror, although you definitely could see your own semi-clouded reflection in it. Its edges were rough, like it was hewn from stone, but the front was flawlessly smooth. It was more like a massive, flat, shiny blue rock, and maybe it was only that.

At exactly 8:30 am, his mother entered his room. He could tell by the way she was walking that the shivah wasn't really over for her. Her movements were unenthusiastic and looked almost robotic. She was carrying a whole new pile of folded laundry and heading towards the closet when she saw it. She froze mid-stride.

"Elisha, what's this doing in your room?"

Keep it simple, he thought and said, "I moved it."

"What do you mean *you* moved it?"

"I mean, I moved it into my room and . . . and . . . I want to keep it in my room."

"Well, do you mind telling me how did YOU get it off the wall?"

"It was easy."

His mother was very dissatisfied with his answer and went in hot pursuit of his father. Shira crawled into the room in the meantime. She was laughing and smiling and oblivious to everything. Elisha stopped to give her a quick hug—any bit of reinforcement would be great before his father stormed in.

Elisha's father also stopped short at the scene. His hands were on his hips looking at the wall.

"Now tell me, Elisha, how exactly did *you* get this ten ton slab off the wall?" he demanded in a sarcastic tone.

Elisha re-enacted his motions with ease, "Just like this."

His parents seemed totally confused and caught off guard, so Elisha knew it was time to take a chance and make good on the moment.

"Mom, Dad, please I want to keep the stone in my room. I know it's worthless, but not to me and . . . ."

His father instantly objected, "Completely out of the question."

"It's absurd looking," his mother complained.

"A monolithic slab in the middle of a 10-year-old's bedroom," his father groaned.

Elisha couldn't help arguing, "But I'm almost 11."

It was the wrong thing to say, and now his mother seemed even more frustrated.

"Your father's right. I'm having it moved out today."

It hadn't gone well at all. His parents were definitely becoming more decisive and against it by the minute. Elisha knew it was war, but instead of raising his voice, he was very surprised to find tears. There was actually a flood of them just waiting for the right moment to pour out.

"But Saba Gabriel gave it to me before he died."

That did it. There was complete silence.

"Don't you dare be disrespectful, Elisha," his father warned.

"I swear it's true."

"Don't you ever swear!" both his parents yelled out at the same time, and with that they left the room together, loudly closing the door. They obviously needed group strategy. Elisha put his ear to the door, but couldn't hear a thing, except that he did catch that usual phrase of theirs, 'overactive imagination'.

But they didn't come back to take away the mirror stone. Not only that, they didn't even mention it again for a long time.

Jonathan waited patiently for Dr. Brody to finish an emergency call, even though he was sure that he was going to lose some of his own paid-for session time in the process.

He couldn't really explain why he hadn't made his own urgent call to the police, especially now that he had Dr. Brody's 'golden seal' of approval. He told himself that it was because of the adverse side effects he was experiencing from the hypnosis. He didn't want to end up being in the untenable situation of suing Dr. Brody for malpractice while submitting those same hypnosis sessions as court evidence. He scanned the awards that Dr. Brody had plastered conspicuously all over his walls, hoping they were legit. He was *supposed* to be the best, and he also charged triple for that accolade. Jonathan had never confronted Dr. Brody with any accusations. He didn't have to. He had researched the subject thoroughly and had easily made his own self-diagnosis. He had the number one side effect resulting from amateur hypnosis, 'psychotic symptoms or acute panic attacks'. Why else would he be freaking out in elevators or seeing bizarre visions in glasses of water? And then there were the *dreams*, which were really nightmares. Every night he was waking up with panic attacks and all he could remember was a crazy sensation of being burnt alive.

When Dr. Brody finally got off the phone, he noticed that Jonathan seemed apprehensive about their upcoming induction.

"Is something wrong?" he casually asked.

Jonathan was thinking, *yeah, you,* but instead he rotated his neck in a circular motion to release his tension and then confidently replied, "No. It's okay, I'm ready to go."

Dr. Brody referred to his file. "Well, the good news is we're making excellent progress and according to my notes we're up to Chamber Four."

Wow. He can count, thought Jonathan, *now maybe he can apply some of that infinite wisdom to his hypnosis skills.*

Dr. Brody still perceived reticence in Jonathan's demeanor. He hesitated momentarily and then asked, "Is there something I should know about Chamber Four, I mean, *before* we start?"

Jonathan replied flatly, "No."

"Well then," Dr. Brody said, "I have one of my own suggestions in order to spend our time more wisely together. I think it would be best if we skipped over all of that chanting that you do at the beginning."

Jonathan cut him off, "You mean the letter permutations incantations?"

"Yes, the mantras—"

"They're *not* mantras. They're *letter permutations*, which means manipulating the letters of the Hebrew alphabet and recombining them into different formulas. It's not the same."

Dr. Brody was annoyed with Jonathan's nitpicking. "Whatever. The point is that it's not necessary to listen to and record all of those . . . ." Dr. Brody so much wanted to say meditation techniques, but he stopped himself and said, "all of those *letter permutation incantations*."

"Why?"

"Well, quite honestly because it's maddeningly *long*."

Jonathan smirked. "You call that *long*? *LONG?*" A large sneer broke out across his face. "Do you know that just on eight letters the amount of possible combinations is 322,560 letters? It really should take 30 *hours*. Twelve letters would take 63 years!" Jonathan's voice became scathing and sarcastic, "In fact, that's one of *Professor Bezalel's* breakthroughs. He figured out compression formulas." Jonathan snorted. "He's a raving lunatic. Do you know that for all 22 letters of the Hebrew alphabet, there's sextillion possible permutations. Do you even know how many that is?"

Dr. Brody looked at him blankly.

"It's the number of stars in the observable universe. So, of course, the madman genius figured out a logarithm to crack that one too."

Dr. Brody still didn't understand what was so important about the letters, and although he hated being on the receiving end of Jonathan's intellectual snobbery, he grumbled, "I still don't see what the point is."

Jonathan raised his eyebrows, as if after making everything so perfectly clear he was in shock that he'd have to repeat himself.

"The letters are *everything*. Think of them like molecular structures of all matter. Manipulate the molecules, and you can manipulate the matter. That's what all of their *maddeningly* long chanting is really about."

Now Dr. Brody raised an eyebrow. Jonathan couldn't possibly be saying that you could change matter with mantras. That would mean what? That you could create things, change objects, perform magic? That was ludicrous. Maybe Jonathan did have FMS.

Jonathan laid his head back on the couch and stared at the spotlights that were set into the ceiling. *Observable stars in the universe? Manipulating matter?* He closed his eyes tight and watched the burned-in spots under his eyelids. He needed to ask himself an important question. *What am I talking about?*

Although he didn't want to admit it, sharing his room with the mirror stone was quite uncomfortable. It gave Elisha the chills, and it wasn't because he was scared or getting sick, or having Bezalel nightmares. Even though it was the middle of the summer, and he owned an overactive imagination, the stone had a weird way of making the whole room ice cold. He grabbed a heavy winter blanket from the top of his closet and laid it on his bed, but then quickly changed his mind and hung it over the mirror instead. A little after 2:00am, he woke up from the freezing cold. He quickly turned on his night table lamp. The bulb instantly burnt out, but it was on long enough for him to see that the blanket had fallen off, and he could feel gusts of icy wind reaching his bed. Frosty as he was, he had no choice but to get up and cover the mirror again more securely.

The first few days after the shivah were also kind of numb. Everyone went about their normal routine, but it was like they were machines. And every night it was the same freezing cold room, but somehow it seemed to get colder with each passing night. No matter how tightly Elisha wrapped the mirror stone, the blanket kept coming off and he'd wake up to the ice age. Of course he didn't dare say a word, and luckily enough, by the morning everything was always back to normal, but Elisha was getting sick and tired of sleeping in Siberia. After all, bedrooms were supposed to be warm and comfortable, especially when life wasn't.

The windowless room was roughly circular. The ceiling was low. You could never tell what time of day it was inside. There was nothing to remind you of the outside, especially not sound. Not even underground sound. When she spoke, she wasn't sure if she had spoken. Unless she kept her eyes open. Then she could see the sound. It was the perfect place to say the letters and watch them. The letters were everything and not letters at all. Not the way people *understood* letters. And never the way people who were somethings used them to talk without saying anything. Or the way they drew them into shapes to explain everything that wasn't wisdom. They had to do it in very straight lines, and with spaces in between and spaces on top, and spaces on the bottom, and rows and rows and rows. She knew they had lots of big rules to keep their understanding in those straight lines with spaces and rows. They never even looked at the wisdom that was left in all of the spaces they had made. That must have been another rule.

She didn't like to look at their dead scribbles, but she could stare forever at the letters of fire that were entire worlds.

She could see them all day long, but only after she first thought of nothing. Then they would fill her entire mind. Then she could see them floating in the air against a blue sky. Then she would watch them through water. The water would get deeper and deeper until they would fade away and all that was left was inky blackness. The blackness would creep over her until she was asleep. Then they became black fire on white fire. And the black fire was as brilliantly black as the white fire was brilliantly white. Then they could all be combined, the way the 'Arranger of Letters' had told them to combine them. Engrave them, cycle them, hew them, combine them, permute them. Engrave them, cycle them, hew them, combine them, permute them. Engrave them, cycle them, hew them, combine them, permute them.

That was the only way to reach the halls.

The 'Arranger of Letters' had showed them how, but he also used those rules sometimes. She never used them, not even once. The 'Arranger of Letters' was fast, but she was *much* faster.

CHAPTER 4

The Night of the 17ᵗʰ of Tammuz

T he night of the 17ᵗʰ of Tammuz fell on a warm Monday night a week after the shivah had ended, and although it was highly unusual for him, Mr. Davidson went into his son's room to say goodnight.

Elisha immediately stiffened, because it usually meant either a lecture or what his father termed a 'pleasant talk'. He braced himself for another stone battle.

His father took his desk chair and placed it to the side of Elisha's bed. He took off his glasses and cleaned them while saying, "Elisha, you do know it's the 17ᵗʰ of Tammuz."

Of course Elisha knew the date. It was *supposed* to be the day that he started Professor Bezalel's Chamber One summer camp, which was probably down the drain now for good and forever. But that, of course, wasn't what his father was referring to. Tomorrow would be a day of mourning and also a fast day for all the adults. The 17ᵗʰ of Tammuz was one of *those* bad dates on the calendar. It was the day that marked the *beginning* of the *end* for both Temples. The day that the fortified stones walls surrounding Jerusalem were breached. Elisha knew that breaking those walls was no easy task; at least not thousands of years ago. The Babylonians had gone through three hundred horses loaded with iron hatchets before they were able to demolish a single gate. The walls were key, because as long as the walls were impenetrable, reaching the Temple would be impossible. But on the 17th of Tammuz, the Babylonians succeeded, and 490 years later on the exact same date, the Romans had ramparted the walls and broken through.

It was also the date that marked a three-week count-down to the only day on the calendar that was considered worse—the dreaded 9th of the month of Av—the exact day of the year when both of the Temples were turned into massive infernos, with their blazing flames burning the magnificent Temples down to the ground, until they were utterly destroyed. It was the day that the soul of the Eternal City was destroyed twice over, and the few survivors that hadn't been massacred were led away in iron chains.

The strange part was the date stayed like that. The 9th of Av *continued* to be catastrophic. Always. Every single disaster had always been on the 9th of Av. From the Spanish Expulsion and right through the Final Solution of the Holocaust, they were all on the 9th of Av. It was a notoriously unlucky day. A day marked by calamities on the Hebrew calendar. It was also Elisha's birthday.

"Now, I know you're not of age yet, but I think it would be a good idea if you tried to fast at least until 1:00 in the afternoon tomorrow, and I also want you to join me for sunrise."

Elisha's father made a regular habit of saying his silent meditation at sunrise at the Kotel—the last remaining wall of the Temple. It was also a short five minute walk from their house. Elisha knew that his father wasn't really asking him, but rather ordering him. Elisha was relieved, and eagerly agreed. As long as they were willing to let him keep the fridge stone, he was ready to cooperate on just about anything.

Right after his father left his room, Elisha tied heavy rope around the blanket in every direction. Once he was satisfied that it would be impossible for it to come off, he went to sleep with the warm summer breeze drifting in through his window.

At 10:00pm, even though he had missed his deadline for work, Jonathan was still at his laptop transcribing every word from his Chamber Four session. He was frantically typing.

> *The Book of Creation tells us everything we need to know about our five dimensional universe. Space has three dimensions; up-down, north-south, and east-west. Six opposite directions. The fourth dimension of time has two directions: past and future or beginning and end. The fifth dimension is the dimension of thought.*

Jonathan stopped. Professor Bezalel was certified *crazy*. You'd think that a physics professor at Cambridge would be a slightly more educated man of science and too enlightened to swallow some sort of thousands-of-years-old ancient Kabbalah textbook postulating a non-existent fifth dimension, or was it even ten? He made another cup of strong coffee for himself and thought of giving it a rest.

He took a sip of the hot caffeine and *remembered* something funny. It was the *Arranger of Letters*—he had typed that out one paragraph ago, and now he remembered it wasn't just about arranging the letters for the permutation incantations—that's how Professor Bezalel called himself in the Chambers. It took all his restraint not to spit out his coffee and burst out laughing. The guy was into giving himself Sesame Street pseudonyms. *Sick.* Jonathan stared at his notes and then slowly composed himself, deciding he'd transcribe for just five minutes more.

> *In the fifth dimension, our physical bodies cannot move at all, but our thoughts can, which is why our bodies need to be entirely stationary first. This is how we must position ourselves. First, we need to sit on the floor, and then see if . . . .*

Jonathan's phone started to buzz incessantly, and he instinctively knew it was his editor, so he didn't answer it. That's when his field of vision dissolved in front of his eyes. *Another panic attack*, but at least he could still hear the phone. Now he really wanted to answer it to ground himself back into reality, but he couldn't see or find the wretched thing, even though he was groping blindly over every surface of his desk.

It stopped buzzing, and his disassembled molecule vision disappeared. He hadn't meant at all to take on the position. It was just natural to sit down on the corner of his bed and to put his head between his knees, except, after that, he wouldn't have to transcribe anything ever again.

He didn't know how long he had been unconscious, but when he came to he knew, without a shadow of a doubt, every single detail of how he had spent *six* summers of his life. Six *whole* summers. It wasn't just some bizarre side effect from the hypnosis. He actually *remembered*. He remembered *everything*.

The crystal clarity of it all was so acute that Jonathan felt sheer empowerment coursing through every part of his body. He raised his hands upward and laughed, moaned, and screamed all at the same time. He had never felt so intensely alive, and his mind was rushing in surges of such forceful energy that he suddenly had to grab the back of his chair for support.

He also felt a sharp rage boiling up inside him that was going to explode. Did they really think they could just erase what *they* started? Delete it all?? Why had they wanted to take *all* of it away from him! Was it because he didn't live up to some sick standard of theirs? Was he defective in some way?? His memory now served him only too well, and Jonathan knew he was their *best*. The best they *ever* had. He laughed and then turned morose again.

Why only *six*!!! Why could he only remember what transpired in six Chambers? He was sure he was a *Seven*, and *Seven* was the quintessence of all the previous Chambers. He *needed* to remember.

He suddenly felt a searing pain in his head, but he didn't care if it burned his brains out. He needed to focus on that seventh summer, on the Seventh Chamber. Focus. *Singular Focus*. The memory of the Seventh Chamber. Jonathan's head shot back from the excruciating pain. He yelled loudly and then stopped. He was too scared. Not of the pain. He was too scared to lose the six precious Chambers he had just regained. The memory of the Seventh seemed firewalled, and the effort to remember it was too difficult. He breathed in deeply while stretching every part of his body and slowly started to relax. OK. He might not be able to remember, but he assured himself that there were lots of *other* ways of getting his Chamber Seven memory back.

Despite Jonathan's innate dislike for Dr. Brody and his profession, he had to acknowledge that his methods had proven to be invaluable.

He thought of his 'old' life's agenda of exposing them. Pathetic. Now, of course, things had changed. The agenda would too. He still wanted to shut them down, but that was only for starters. He'd make that call to the police tomorrow, and Dr. Brody would be easily manipulated and would continue filling in the blanks for him.

Right now, there was only one word in that blank, empty space of his mind. Jerusalem. His seventh memory was there. The ancient city was calling him.

When he had moved to Tel Aviv four years before, he had sworn that he would *never* go back to Jerusalem for *anything*, ever. Tomorrow was a good day to break vows. He didn't have to consult a Hebrew calendar to know what day it was. Some things would always remain reflex.

Like clockwork, at 2:00 am, Elisha woke up from the cold, but this time he was so frozen he could barely move. His T-shirt even felt as stiff as ice. *How could the blanket have possibly fallen this time?* He didn't even bother turning on the light, but then something scared him even stiffer. It was his father's footsteps coming toward his room. That would be the end of it, he was sure. The door opened and light poured into his room. Why in the world would his father be coming into his room at this hour? They had at least three more hours to sleep. He didn't dare even look at the mirror stone. His father was coming toward his bed. He couldn't think up one good excuse and just pretended to be asleep. His father's hand brushed the top of his head. *That was weird.* Then he realized that he was trying to feel his forehead for a temperature.

"Elisha, Elisha," his father was gently shaking him and whispering, "are you alright? You're sweating. Your forehead is a bit hot too."

Hot, HOT?? What in the world was he saying? Did he just confuse the words? It took all of Elisha's might to stop his body from shivering and his teeth from chattering from the ice cold. He answered sleepily, "I'm not hot."

Jessie Davidson was scratching the side of his neck. It was a swelteringly hot night. Central AC was next on Tamar's list. Maybe she had a point. He opened the window over Elisha's bed until its hinges met the back wall and said quietly, "OK, go back to sleep . . . ."

What a relief! The minute he could tell that the footsteps were back in their own room, Elisha got to his feet, but when he did he had to hold back an aching scream. He was sure that the floor of his room had been transformed into a sheet of dry ice, and now his feet were stuck to the surface. He was in agony and held his head tight with his hands. Then there was the loudest clunk. Elisha couldn't make out much in the darkness, but he was sure that a piece of the stone had fallen onto the floor; either that or it had turned into an automatic ice machine. He reached for the night table lamp, but realized it was blown out. That's when the silent earthquake started, and it was so violent that Elisha's vision became stripes of blurred and chaotic movement. He was screaming, but nothing was coming out. His voice was broken—just a frosty scrape of tongue against throat.

The earthquake had managed to obliterate his room; he was left standing isolated in a space of zero-ness. The only familiar object left in his room was the mirror stone.

A black fiery light suddenly captured his attention, but he was paralyzed. It was growing wider and twisting like a cyclone. There was also something wrong with his vision. He was seeing colors that didn't exist. Fire couldn't be black, but it was. Or was he seeing it reversed and negative? It was as if everything he had known about colors had been stripped away and he could see them as they really were. Here they were different intensities of energy, a new and wider spectrum, and the colors had *sounds*. Weird sounds.

Elisha shut his eyes tight to make everything disappear. A feverish chain of thoughts attacked his mind: His father didn't feel the cold, and there was probably no snake-like black fire now. Saba Gabriel never made him promise anything. Professor Bezalel never stared at him. Maybe his room was catching on fire, maybe his father was right about it being hot. He opened his eyes hoping for a change of scenery. There was. The black fire cyclone was getting longer and longer, and within it a white liquidy fire was appearing and swirling into shapes. He closed his eyes again, but saw the exact image even with his eyes shut tight. It was then that he decided he might as well keep his eyes open, and then nothing could stop him from staring at the amazing sight, until it finally occurred to him that the white fire on the black fire was forming into letters, and that somewhere in the background there was a voice, a still small voice. It was a familiar voice, but was it his own? Maybe it was his lungs wheezing as they breathed in and out the ice cold air? It was getting louder, but, he wasn't only hearing it, he was *seeing* it. He couldn't explain how, but he was seeing *sound*. Or maybe it was sound waves, but they were there and they filled his entire non-existent room. There were words being said and seen, but he couldn't understand them. Now the voice was clear and unmistakable; it was his own. He was reading the glowing black fiery words that were tornadoing out of the stone and being etched on to the mirror in ancient Hebrew script, or were they reflecting off the mirror, or being etched under his eyelids? It was dizzying and disorienting, but they there were: *17th of Tammuz, 5777. Find the Kohen of Light*.

A blinding burst of invisible color with a humming sound scarred his eyes, then it ignited more black and white fire, and again the letters formed, '*17th of Tammuz, 5777. Find the Kohen of Light*'. Elisha found himself repeating after a disembodied voice that he could *see*, a voice that had once put him to sleep with story after story, a voice that was sorely missed now, a voice that was supposed to be silent. Another earthquake hit the room and then the mirror stone sucked everything away, the whirlwinds of black, rivers of white fire, the strange spectrum of shrieking colors, the wild sound waves. Everything was gone.

Elisha was shaking and trembling, but the sentence kept repeating itself over and over again in his head, '*17th of Tammuz, 5777. Find the Kohen of Light*'. It was like it had been indelibly imprinted on his mind, and he would never have any other thought again for the rest of his life. He was also running out of his room now with his heart in his throat. He needed to find out if there were any survivors left in his family. '*17ᵗʰ of Tammuz, 5777. Find the Kohen of Light*'. He practically smashed right into his mother in the hallway and shouted out in panic.

"ARE YOU OKAY? *17ᵗʰ of Tammuz 5777. Find the Kohen of Light.*" What had he *said*? Without hearing the colors and seeing the sound, the sentence was suddenly distorted and unrecognizable.

She looked at him thoroughly confused and asked in an exhausted voice, "Are *you* okay?"

Some remote part of Elisha's mind that wasn't thinking, '*17ᵗʰ of Tammuz, 5777. Find the Kohen of Light*', suddenly grasped that everything might have stayed normal outside of his room, because he heard Shira crying and saw that his mother looked totally regular and had a bottle in her hand.

Elisha's father practically fell into the hallway and asked in alarm, "*WHAT* happened!!??"

Elisha's heart was still racing when he said, "THE EARTHQUAKE! I wanted to make sure that everyone was OKAY!"

His parents exchanged meaningful looks.

"You take care of the baby," his mother said as she handed the bottle to his father with one hand, while she took Elisha's hand in her other. "It was just a nightmare, sweetheart," she said as she hugged him. "Let's get you back into bed".

He got it then. It was just *him*.

His mother sat down next to him on the bed and fluffed up his pillow. "You want to tell me about it?"

He did. He felt he had to, even if it was just pretending that it was his dream. His heart was still beating fast as the strange images tumbled out. "There was an earthquake and strange colors, and black fire and Saba was telling me something. I couldn't see him, but I saw the words he was saying."

Even as the words left his mouth, Elisha was aware that he was doing a terrible job of describing what had happened. It sounded like a bad dream to him too. It also took a huge effort not to keep repeating, '17ᵗʰ *of Tammuz, 5777. Find the Kohen of Light*'.

His mother looked calmly and lovingly at him and said again, "It was only a nightmare, sweetheart. Try to forget about it and get back to sleep." But Tamar Davidson was also looking at the mirror stone. She had very keen instincts of her own and somehow felt that the stone was suspect. "Do you get the feeling, Elisha, that it has something to do with that?" she pointed at the wall.

Elisha said nothing and closed his eyes. His mother kissed his cheek. He wanted to tell her to stay in his room and to sleep next to him tonight. He really wanted to say that and not '17ᵗʰ *of Tammuz, 5777. Find the Kohen of Light*'.

His mother stayed on the edge of his bed for about 10 minutes more, and when she thought he was asleep, she quietly left the room. Elisha waited a few seconds more and then got right up. He ran to his bedroom door and turned on the ceiling light in his room.

Everything looked so perfectly normal, like a seven-scale earthquake hadn't even taken place. He could still see clear traces of the fiery script under his eyelids. What did it mean? Why was it assaulting his brain? *Now* was the 17ᵗʰ of Tammuz. It had started tonight and would continue until tomorrow after sunset. It was also the year 5777 on the Hebrew calendar. But who was the Kohen or Priest of Light, and how in the world was he supposed to find one? He stared at the familiar things in his room and wished there was some kind of evidence to prove what had happened was real. He went to check the stone; it looked its usually slabby mirror-smooth self and nothing more than a stone. He was crouching alongside the bottom of it when he suddenly froze from hearing a different sound. It was the sound of loud voices fighting, and they belonged to his parents.

Elisha never *ever* remembered hearing his parents raise their voices at each other like *that* before. In seconds, it managed to darken all of his excitement. He stiffened on the spot and barely breathed so that he could catch something of what they were saying. Everything was muffled, but his father was very angry and his mother was crying hard. He definitely did hear one word loudly enough and clearly enough, and it was all he needed to know. It was his name. He didn't want to hear any more, and he ran back into his bed.

His head was spinning wondering why his parents would be fighting about *him*? He could still hear it from here. Now his mother was the one yelling. It was probably why his father had come into the room the first time. Maybe they were right to be screaming about him. He had probably lost his mind and they were fighting over which institution to send him away to. He could envision it perfectly. His mother was crying because she probably wanted to take care of her insane son at home, but his father was insisting that he had to *go*, and then he'd spend the rest of his life in a padded cell just repeating, '17th *of Tammuz, 5777. Find the Kohen of Light*'. He was staring at the door as if that could help him hear their voices any better, and that's when he suddenly noticed that a piece of the mirror stone *was* lying on the floor under his desk. Elisha jumped to the spot in seconds. He quickly looked back at the stone again—there weren't any pieces missing. He reached for the smooth object and then practically threw it across the room. He didn't know what to feel first: the fact that it had burned his hand or that he was totally stunned at what he had seen. He ran over to the spot where he had flung it, and all he could do was to stare, blink and stare, and continue to gape while his mind raced with thoughts.

He had *seen* pictures of this exact stone in Professor Bezalel's class. It actually wasn't a stone at all, but rather a large beautifully cut greenish-blue gem with ancient Hebrew writing etched artfully through it. His imagination was definitely not running away with him, and he felt sure that he recognized the object. As impossible as it seemed, this gem looked just the way a Choshen stone should look: One of the twelve stones from the High Priest's breastplate. It was exactly like the diagrams they had studied all year long, and it wasn't just theory and pictures.

The mid-term class project had required each of them to make a clay replica of one of the stones, and Professor Bezalel made a student redo it if it wasn't up to specifications. Elisha lay down on the floor and positioned his face as close as he could get to it without getting burnt. It was *exactly* the right size. This stone had the name of the tribe of Judah clearly and beautifully etched in ancient Hebrew letters, which were glowing as if a fire was within the jewel and lighting them from behind. It was like staring straight into an optical illusion, because he could see that the letters read correctly on both sides, even though they looked like they went all the way through the gem on each side. How *did* they do that?

Elisha knew. Just about everything important in

the Temple was made using a Shamir. Tools were never allowed to touch these things, which was impossible when you thought about it because how could you make anything without them? But tools were definitely *not* allowed—something about them being used for war and bloodshed would somehow ruin the Temple's essence of peace. But *no one* even knew what a Shamir was. Professor Bezalel didn't know either. He had told them it was either a living creature or a radioactive substance. Elisha felt like screaming. He was sure he was right. He wanted to shout out to the whole world his amazing discovery. He thought of quickly running to Professor Bezalel, the only person on the face of the earth who would know, and how his face would light up like rocket fuel to see it. It seemed so cruel that Professor Bezalel with his amnesia wouldn't even care. He wished so much that he could go running to his parents right now too. Maybe seeing the sparkling gem would distract them and make them happy again. He was sure they were probably fighting because he had told them about the earthquake. *No.* It would be the mirror stone's death sentence. He stared again at the beautiful turquoise-colored gem. He couldn't think of a living soul that he could even share his amazing secret with, now that Saba Gabriel was gone. He heard himself whispering the message again, '*17ᵗʰ of Tammuz, 5777. Find the Kohen of Light*'. He was scared. He felt all the hair follicles on his body bristling.

He stopped. He had to get a hold of himself and stop saying that sentence. He needed to be like his father—analytical and logical. *Think!* If it really was one of the 12 stones from the Choshen, then only a High Priest could touch it. But where in the world was he supposed to find this Kohen Priest of Light?? Who do you go to?

Who do you ask, if you couldn't Google something? *Who do you ask?*

All of a sudden there was no doubt in Elisha's mind; he had to find that strange man with the Choshen calling card—Rav Yehuda Kadosh. It just could *not* be a coincidence. Didn't his father say that he was a great Mekubal? Who else but a Kabbalah master would know how to deal with a situation like this?

He ran to his desk to find the 'business card' he had given him, but he couldn't find a thing among the mess of strewn candy wrappers, empty plastic cups, and pencil shavings. When he did find it, the back side was glued to his desk with something sticky and he had to peel it off, losing whatever layer of back cover was there. He flipped through the small book of Tehillim again. There was no address to be found. Not on the inside cover, not anywhere. He tried to read the page that had stuck to his desk, but it wasn't there either.

The burns on his hand suddenly hurt like crazy. One spot was already starting to blister.

Elisha decided to sneak off to the kitchen to grab some equipment and supplies. He carefully opened his door. A flood of the fighting noises came through again and mixed in with *17th of Tammuz, 5777. Find the Kohen of Light.* He let the message in his brain play at maximum volume so he could block out their yelling. He grabbed a package of frozen peas, BBQ tongs, and two fluffy potholder mitts. It took both mitts to even be able to handle the gem, and then he wrapped a small towel around both the gem and the potholders. Elisha forced the bulky bundle into his black camping pouch, which could barely zipper, and with that accomplished he climbed back into bed, laying the package of frozen peas over his burnt hand. The pouch felt like a nice warm hot water bottle as it rested against his chest. He pulled his sheet over his head. His mind was made up. Rav Kadosh would have the answers. It was the only thought that let him fall back to sleep for another two hours.

Jonathan couldn't sleep. He went to look at himself in the mirror. A part of him knew what he was now: He was separate from the rest, entirely different. Yet his reflection was hiding this fact. *That was good.* He started touching his face. Hands. People thought they knew what they could do with their hands. Not *these* hands. He even thought he understood why they had done it. He washed his hands carefully and clipped off his fingernails as low as he could. He gathered every single clipping and flushed them down the toilet. He knew this was essential. He needed to keep to certain rules, at least for now. He checked his watch. It was 3:30 am. Four years was a long time. He urgently needed to make complete body contact with an element that was as old as creation itself. It was a ten minute walk to the Tel Aviv beach. It was deserted. He took off all of his clothes, along with his ring and watch, and then dove deep into the warm black nighttime waves of the Mediterranean Sea without the slightest fear. He immersed himself seven times until he could feel the surge of energy from the all-encompassing primordial contact.

Now he would break every rule in the book.

CHAPTER 5

THE 17th of Tammuz

At 5:00 am Elisha heard his father's chorus of alarm clocks ringing. He was still holding the pouch tightly to his chest. He was up in a split second. It was still real.

Mr. Davidson forced a smile for his young son getting up on time, but his own face showed that he was exhausted.

"I'm so glad that on such an important day, you're making the appropriate effort," he said as he helped Elisha organize himself.

Elisha tried acting as normal as possible, as if he didn't have a Choshen stone in his pouch, and as if he wasn't carrying the pain of his parents fighting about him all night. His father seemed too tired to talk about anything, and Elisha thought that was good. He really didn't want to be sent away to some mental institution before seeing Rav Kadosh.

He followed dutifully at his father's side as they made their way through the Jerusalem stone alleyways of the nearly-deserted Old City. Their feet made light tapping sounds on the stones as they quietly walked along. The noises were still nighttime noises. So, Elisha practically whispered his desperate question.

"Dad. Do you remember that man that visited us on the last day of the shivah, the one you kept calling a great Mekubal?"

His father yawned, and then answered quietly, "Remember? Who could forget?"

"Well, is he from Jerusalem?"

His father was quick to respond, and there was even a tinge of enthusiasm in his tired voice.

"Elisha, *that* man isn't just a great Mekubal; he's the *greatest* and last remaining Mekubal we have today. He's a giant, a living legend in our own time."

Elisha knew he couldn't possibly be a giant height-wise.

His father continued. "Did you know that he never, *ever* leaves the Wall, which is why we were *so* shocked to see him at the shivah."

Elisha could hear the disbelief in his father's voice as he recounted it, but Elisha was just thrilled to find out that the Mekubal was *minutes* away.

"And by the way, it's a well-documented fact that he hasn't left his room at the Wall in over 40 years. Can you imagine *that*? That's why his followers call him 'The Guardian'." His father yawned loudly and added, "Believe me, everyone's still clueless as to why he came out for Saba Gabriel's shivah. The whole Old City was spinning up speculations right, left, and center about that one." He did a double yawn and then added, "I only wish *I* knew."

Elisha's only focus was to find out where the Mekubal's lifetime headquarters were. He asked curiously, "So where does he stay?"

Elisha's father wasn't paying attention to him.

"You should know that I once had the privilege of

working with him on a very rare Kabbalah manuscript from Ferarra, Italy, dating back to the 16ᵗʰ century. A Kadosh family heirloom."

Elisha could tell the conversation was going to become very academic if he didn't quickly shift the conversation back on track. "Which room is it?" Elisha asked, while scanning along with his father the view of the Western Wall Plaza that was now sprawling out in front of them, still brightly lit up from the streetlamps.

His father pointed to a blocky Jerusalem-stone building with narrow windows that was directly to the left of the Wall. "It's right up there, near the Kotel Rav's quarters, second floor."

Elisha thought he couldn't have had better luck. He knew exactly where he needed to go, even though he had never been inside the building before.

There was no more conversation as they reached the midway lookout point. It didn't matter how many times you descended the steps, the scene was always spectacular. The silhouette of the ages, the last remaining wall of the Temple was looming directly ahead of them. Elisha thought his heart would burst. Here he was holding a Choshen stone, just at the right place, and only two or three thousand years off. Maybe just reaching the Wall with his pouch would be enough to find the *Kohen of Light*, but then he reminded himself that the real spot would be behind it, where the golden Dome of the Rock Mosque was standing. He wondered about going there. He had never stepped foot on the other side, but he also knew it was way too dangerous. Then his feet stopped short as he stared straight at the security checkpoint that was directly in front of him. He hadn't thought about having to go *through* security with his pouch.

The heavily guarded security checkpoint had its regular group of soldiers and police officers working around the clock to ensure there were no terrorist attacks on the #1 target—the last remnant of the Second Temple and its crowds of praying visitors. *All* bags *always* had to go through the metal detector and X-ray machine, *no* exceptions. His father noticed his hesitation and asked, "What's the matter?"

Elisha automatically answered, "I forgot I brought my pouch."

"So what? Just put it on the conveyer belt."

And before Elisha could say a thing, his father was already helping him to do it. Elisha could barely breathe as he watched his pouch disappear into the black hole of the X-ray machine. *It better come out, and it better not look weird to the security guy.* But it did. He stopped the belt. Elisha's eyes were staring straight at the security officer whose eyes were looking intently at a monitor.

"What's in your bag?" he demanded.

Elisha felt a nervous sweat break out, but knew he couldn't tell the truth. "It's a game," he answered, but his voice sounded full of it and for some reason he also knew that he was wearing the guiltiest face in the world. When he tried to wipe it off, he felt it was looking worse by the second.

The security guard obviously noticed and immediately came out with his second demand. "Open the bag and take it out."

It was just then that Elisha's father came to the rescue. "Natan, it's fine. He's my son."

The security guy looked up and then instantly relaxed. There was a very warm smile on his face when he said, "Jessie, I haven't seen you in a while."

Elisha's father offered back a tired smile, "And I was just thinking that you haven't been on the graveyard shift for months."

Natan had forgotten all about Elisha's pouch at that point and was more interested in making conversation. "Is this really your kid?" he asked curiously.

"I know, I know . . . he looks like his mother, but yes, this is my oldest, Elisha."

Elisha was wondering why that sounded like an apology, when the security guy tisked. "Well Jessie, you certainly know better," he said, nodding to Elisha's father to 'take care of the matter'. And with that, he handed the unsearched pouch right back into Elisha's hands.

Elisha thought he could have fainted with relief. One thing was for sure; he'd never make a good terrorist or spy. Then just as they left the security checkpoint, his father pulled him to the side.

"You did hear what he said, right?" He looked down very seriously at Elisha and added, "Next time leave that ridiculous pouch at home." He motioned him to start walking toward the Wall, but the lecture mood was still in full force. "I just can't even comprehend it. You come down to the Wall—*The Kotel*—with a computer game? Really, Elisha! Honestly, it's embarrassing . . . and on a day like today!"

Well, there was nothing for Elisha to say, so he just kept silent. But if his father only *knew*. No more words were spoken on the matter as Mr. Davidson and Elisha made their way across the wide stone plaza, and nothing needed to be said for Elisha to sense his father's tired and aggravated mood.

Even at this early hour, there was already a fair amount of people gathering at the Wall. The 17th of Tammuz was *one* of those dates where you could expect a larger turnout, and it would grow as the day progressed.

They had barely entered the perimeter of the Wall itself when another one of those 'sonic booms' cracked and jolted them. Elisha nearly jumped out of his skin. He had been on edge anyways because of the security check, but what had really set him off was that he had *seen* the audio waves of that sonic boom, and they were freakier-looking than any of the ones that had been in his bedroom last night. He also noticed something else strange. Only a handful of people had reacted to the sound. Elisha felt like he had watched in slow motion as just a few heads broke from the crowd, slightly lost their balance and grasped at the air, searched the sky, and then looked at other people around them to confirm what had happened. Elisha's father was one of them. Elisha didn't need to think too hard about it now. The last time he had heard that noise was on the day that the mirror stone was found. His heart started beating wildly. *What if it kept happening and they got even stronger?*

Jessie Davidson knew that there was no such thing as a selective sonic boom, and while he didn't show it, this time the sound set off a red alert in his mind. A high one. He'd have to go. He looked down at Elisha and assured himself that there wasn't a safer place to leave him. He took out his phone and pretended to study a message while saying, "Elisha, I'm sorry, but I'm going to have to go. Something has come up."

He surveyed the plaza, "You'll be fine. Just join my quorum, and if you don't see me, then head home right after."

Elisha was feeling mixed. It wasn't the first time his father had received one of these emergency calls, and a part of him couldn't have been happier to be left on his own, but he didn't like the thought of his father actually leaving him alone, especially if the world was going to come crashing down on his head.

Elisha stood in the middle of the plaza and watched his father walk away. He was almost entirely out of sight, and there hadn't been any more sonic booms. Elisha convinced himself that it was safe enough and then ran off quickly in pursuit of the Mekubal.

Jonathan was walking aimlessly through the darkened Jerusalem alleyways that he had once cursed. He felt a seething anger rising with every step he took. Six years of tedious work were bound up with every stone and every flashing memory, but what good was powerful knowledge if you didn't have something tangible to go along with it? *And why didn't he? WHY?* Something wasn't making sense. He could *feel* the city's energy buffering him on all sides, but it was eluding him and teasing him, and more than anything, it was *enraging* him because he couldn't *connect* with it. He descended the stairs to the Western Wall Plaza. The energy was even stronger here. As he walked toward the Wall, he was immediately accosted with outstretched palms that were relentlessly pressing in on him. Jonathan dodged them, thinking that every one of these beggars were just trying to outdo the other with their well-rehearsed lines . . . a dying wife, a child who needed a kidney transplant, a man without legs, a blind person . . . yaddah yaddah. But then he stopped. The beggars stopped along with him, thinking he was about to reach into his pocket, but he wasn't. He suddenly felt a grip of fear that knocked all the breath out of him. He stood paralyzed, unable to take a step closer to the Wall. Something he couldn't see was physically pushing him back. He tried moving forward again, but it was as if a solid metal wall was directly in front of him. He stepped to the right and tried again. The sensation of being pushed back was getting stronger. Without turning around, he started taking steps backwards. He knew he didn't look strange because, in any case, that was the custom when one walked away from the Wall. You didn't 'turn your back' on it.

The minute Jonathan was at a safe distance, he turned around and walked slowly away from the plaza area. He was *not* going to be pushed around and had no intention of being cheated out of what he rightfully deserved. He just needed more *time*. He would spend all day here if that's what it took to re-bond to this over-whelmingly forceful place and regain his mastery. He looked back at the crowds of people trying to get their turn at touching the Wall and felt utterly disgusted. Let the idiots fast; he was going to get himself a big breakfast.

Elisha found the arched stone entrance to the building right away. But at dusk, without any lights on, it looked like a dark, uninviting cavity. There was a narrow stone staircase which led into pitch-black darkness. Elisha had no choice but to feel his way up, which he wasn't too happy about. The ancient stone walls on both sides were cold and slightly damp despite the warmth outside.

He had already climbed up what felt like at least two flights in the blackness when he started losing his nerve. He couldn't even see his hands in front of his face. How many more stairs would he have to go up in the dark? He knew his mother would have never let him venture into this major safety hazard, and why would anybody be there now anyways? *Dad had said he was always here.* Then it occurred to him that it would probably be harder and more dangerous going down. Alright, he told himself, *ten more steps max, and if there's nothing, I'll turn around.* But there weren't any more steps. His forehead hit a wall in front of him. *Dead end.* He quickly turned around in the darkness and couldn't understand why his hands were feeling solid wall in this direction too. He must not have turned in the right direction. He grasped at the sides, they were solid wall too. He had walked into a coffin of solid stone on all sides! He suppressed a deep scream, and then realized he should let it out. He kicked his feet in every direction, but there was no opening or stairs to be found. He even heard himself let out a small whimper. That's when he lost it and started pounding the walls with his fists, and screaming full force for help, but it was like his screams were completely deafened by the sealed tomb. He checked his pockets feeling for the stone. It was still there and still warm. His hands also touched another object: It was the small Tehillim that Rav Kadosh had given him. *Nothing to help him escape.* He continued pounding every surface his hands could reach, with the most desperate thoughts for someone to save him.

That was just before he suddenly felt like the biggest idiot. His panicked fumbling had activated a light, and now it was just ridiculously obvious that he had found his way into a small elevator. Of course there was no exit, he stupidly thought to himself, but why didn't he remember hearing any elevator doors closing? He calmly got a grip on his overactive imagination and coolly inspected the elevator buttons. There was only one and he pressed it. The elevator lurched upward for what seemed to be another two flights. *This is fine. This is normal.*

When the elevator door opened, Elisha was startled to see a smiling Rav Kadosh already waiting for him. He summoned Elisha into a small high-ceilinged room made entirely of ancient Jerusalem stone. The walls were packed full of very old-looking books that were unraveling at their seams, and two simple wood chairs and a desk stood in the middle. There were no windows, but the room was as bright as the outdoors.

"Welcome, Elisha, I didn't know it would be so soon. I'm glad you understood how to use my calling card."

Elisha looked down at the Tehillim, and then at Rav Kadosh.

Rav Kadosh wasted no time. "You've come to me with lots of questions, and quite honestly, my boy, I do not have the answers. You might have done something very special as a child that you're not even aware of, although I doubt it, or more than likely, it's simply something you were born with. DNA works in mysterious ways. Actually, I think it was in the merit of your great-ancestors, or very possibly your mother, a very special woman. In any case, I don't know why it's *you*."

Elisha definitely sensed total puzzlement in that last remark. Rav Kadosh paused as if he didn't want to say more, but then slowly continued.

"There's a time for everything, Elisha, but I'm not sure that this is necessarily the right time, although it will be hastened when it is."

Elisha didn't want to be disrespectful, but what was he going on about? He tried to interrupt.

"Rav Kadosh, if you'll excuse me please . . . ."

But Rav Kadosh was having a one-way conversation. "I know your birthday is coming up, dreadful day as it is to be born on, but then again, we don't choose those days, do we? Or the fact that you did not need the mark of the covenant, and that you almost died as a child."

Okay. *What on earth is he talking about?* He must have thought he was someone else. Everything was all *wrong*, except for his birthday. It was bizarrely embarrassing, and Elisha instantly understood that Rav Kadosh was a bit . . . .

"All building blocks. Yes, yes, good building blocks. And here you are. The *Yessod. The one who connects.*"

Elisha was regretting his decision. He lowered his head and stared at the pouch that held his prize possession. He wouldn't even think of sharing his secret with Rav Bizarro.

"Well, Elisha, I'm a very busy man, and I'm sure you can understand that it's prohibited for me to leave my post."

What post was that? Elisha wondered. He started having an overwhelming urge to run out of the room. "Rav Kadosh, I . . . I . . . ," Elisha wasn't sure how to find a good enough excuse to leave respectfully, but the Rav finished the sentence for him.

"Need to find a Kohen of Light?"

Elisha was stunned. His heart started beating wildly. The Rav *knew*. He had found help.

Rav Kadosh was unfazed. "Yes, you made quite a grand entrance with your Choshen stone 13 minutes ago. At least it didn't take the Wall down. And as for your task at hand, don't let the light part confuse you, Elisha. Your job today is to *simply* find a Kohen."

Elisha was instantly relieved. Well that wasn't hard; there were Kohanim all over the place. On his street alone there were two Kohen families, even his best friend Josh Kohen was a Kohen, and there were tons of them to be found in the Old City. You could also easily find them in groups because there was a priestly blessing given every day.

He was heartened. "Well, that should be easy then, right?"

Suddenly, Rav Kadosh burst out laughing a hearty deep chuckle. He laughed so hard that Elisha felt terrified. *What was so funny?* The Rav quickly composed himself.

"Elisha, we all know that there are people with the *name* Kohen or Katz, or even Azouly, on every street corner. The problem is," and he stood up for effect, "I'm not sure if even one of them is a *true* Kohen. The priestly lines have completely deteriorated over the generations and thousands of years. I can't honestly say for sure if there is even *one* Kohen left in our days that is a *direct* descendant of Moses' brother, Aaron."

Elisha sighed, no wonder he had a laughing seizure, but a sudden determination came over him. "Saba Gabriel said to find one—that means there has to be one!"

The statement obviously caught the Rav off guard. He repeated the name 'Gabriel' to himself as if he had to figure out a new mystery. The Rav was pleased. "That's the spirit, my boy, and you don't have much time to find one, so you better start looking."

Now came the tactics part, and the Rav took on the persona of a general. "Start downstairs at the Wall itself, go from quorum to quorum, but make sure you come back at least twice today. Don't forget that there are two priestly blessings today, in the morning and afternoon, and you must find the Kohen *today*, on the 17th of Tammuz, *before* the end of the fast. That will give you until 8:03 tonight. Make sure you cover the main sanctuaries—Yochanan Ben Zakai, The Hurva, Elijah the Prophet, The Kahal Tziyon, Kabbalists Beit El, Midrash Hakotel, and don't rule out those Americans and Canadians at Isralight and Aish, you never know."

Elisha's head was spinning. There were enough priestly blessings going on in a 10 minute radius to keep him busy for a week.

The Rav read his mind. "You'd better get going. The Three Weeks have started and your catastrophic birthday is around the corner."

Elisha's eyes widened, and then Rav Kadosh made him feel even more apprehensive.

"And *my* singular question is, will we be mourning or celebrating when it arrives?"

Elisha looked up at him in alarm, and then became shocked by what he saw. Rav Kadosh suddenly looked like he had doubled in age. Or was it the light?

The Rav stood up and then asked with an intensely powerful voice, "BUT THE MOST important question is, *where* is the *Shamir*?"

Elisha became terrified and confused. "I, I didn't get a Shamir with it."

The Rav's face started collapsing under its wrinkles, and then he practically pushed Elisha out through a different door. Elisha was disoriented.

"Where's the elevator?"

The Rav's aging face was amused. His voice cracked, "Here? An elevator?"

But Elisha wasn't ready to leave yet. He had at least a million questions left and was now stammering to just get out the most important ones.

"Wait, wait, how will I know if I've found the right Kohen?"

"The stone will know," said the Rav quickly, as he started shutting the door on Elisha.

"And what do I do when I find him?" Elisha desperately blurted out.

The Rav was growing older by the second and was very disturbed to have to answer the obvious. "Give him the stone, of course! Do I have to say bippity boppity boo for you to understand?!"

Elisha practically shouted out his panic, "I don't understand any of this!"

But the door was slammed closed and was also marked with a 'no entrance' sign on it. Elisha couldn't understand why after such a warm welcome, the Rav was desperate to get rid of him, but, at least this exit had a well-lit staircase.

Back at the Kotel plaza, the sun was now rising, and Elisha searched the gathering crowd for Kohanim. He approached one of the quorums and paid attention to the leader. Perfect timing. They were almost at the point of the priestly blessing. Elisha felt his heart beating *17th of Tammuz, 5777. Find the Kohen of Light.* This was chance number one.

But, it was trickier than he had figured. First, you were never supposed to look at the Kohanim when they were raising their hands during the chant, and most people even turned to the side so they wouldn't even look by accident. And, secondly, as a precaution, the priests were all covered up under their *tallitot*. Elisha snuck a sideways glance, but they just looked like a ghostly group all huddled together. Elisha knew that underneath their tent-like space, their arms were extended with their hands spread out and their fingers were separated into two groups. Elisha tried to position his hands like the priests. You had to keep a space between your middle and fourth fingers and move them to the side. It was one of those hard things to do that you had to practice, kind of like reaching your tongue to your nose. He wondered what people would think if he tried to go up to them now? *No. It wouldn't work.* Then he got an idea. The Kohanim always went out to ritually wash their hands before the blessing. He could easily find each quorum's priests there. He quickly moved to the area that held the stone basin sink, and since the hall entrance was narrow, each one of them would have to pass by him, but nothing, absolutely nothing happened. *What's supposed to happen anyways?* Was he supposed to go up to each one and ask them if they were missing something?

He felt stupid, and started thinking up even stupider things to do. Once he tried staring at each priest, then he closed his eyes and randomly opened them to find the right one, then he counted to 17 and did the same. He even tried listening carefully to the priests, thinking there might be a hidden message coming from one of the Kohanim, but the chant, of course, was always the same. And it was short—only three sentences and a total of 15 words. Elisha knew the priestly blessing by heart. He also knew that archaeologists had found those 15 words in lots of places. They were etched into rocks, and they had even found two silver scrolls with them in a nearby tomb. Now he was amazed to think that this thousands-of-years-old chant was as old as his stone, although absolutely no hidden messages came his way, except the one that was still imprinted in his brain: *17th of Tammuz, 5777. Find the Kohen of Light.*

This time Ezra was the one that, thankfully, stood up for her, and Ezra knew how to be adamant and get his way.

"I'm sorry, Dr. Allon, but we honestly don't care about your scheduling difficulties. I will repeat that under *no* circumstances will we consent for my brother-in-law to undergo the third surgery today."

Rebecca stood up straight by his side, holding her aching back, and emphatically nodding her agreement. It was infuriating how this misogynist doctor treated her like she was some weak, indecisive person just because she was pregnant.

Dr. Allon gave them both a condescending look. "Let's be honest then. The only reason why you won't agree is because of today's *date*."

It took them both a second to react. It was true that they hadn't expected him to be aware of the Hebrew date.

Dr. Allon added in a sarcastic tone, "I know the date, and I also know that backwards superstitions hold no statistical weight in modern medicine."

At that, Ezra could barely hold back his anger. "Let me get this straight. Yesterday, when he was supposed to urgently have the surgery and even YOU said he couldn't wait another day, *you* delayed it for the sake of convenience, and *today*, you will totally and disrespectfully tread on an ancient tradition, once again for the sake of your own convenience."

Dr. Allon was about to respond when a fourth voice surprisingly entered the conversation.

"I want the surgery today." It was Daniel.

Ezra and Rebecca quickly went to his side, but they were at a loss of how to explain the situation.

Dr. Allon was quick to smile. "Good. Then it's decided." He signaled to an attending intern, while making a confident exit and adding, "I'm glad that there's one clear thinker amongst us."

Ezra was at Daniel's bedside, gesturing anxiously with his hands in all directions, and wearing an expression of 'it's useless', but he still said, "Daniel. It's the *17th of Tammuz!*"

He flatly responded, "So??"

Rebecca and Ezra exchanged glances. How could they fill in the holes? How could they explain that this was once one of the *most important* days on his calendar? He would never have even given the slightest consideration to partake in something as risky as *surgery* on such an ominous day.

Rebecca bit her lip in irritation and then she hit her brother on the arm. She knew it was childish, but she had to do something with her pent-up frustration. Ezra understood. He wanted to hit something too. The thing was that when little sisters grew up, you still couldn't hit them back. He tried doing something constructive instead. He leaned close towards Daniel's face and looked at him straight in the eyes.

"Daniel. Today . . . the 17th of Tammuz. You'd be opening the Chambers Program. Does that ring a bell?" He repeated himself slowly, "*The Chambers Program.*"

"Look, my head isn't functioning," Daniel said as he rubbed his temples and his eyelids drooped uncontrollably.

They could tell that he was weak and in pain, so they were surprised when he tried making an effort to remember.

"Chambers . . . Chambers . . . maybe, there is something, but was I a judge or a barrister in these chambers?"

Nothing had come out of anything. The four Sephardi services in the Old City were all also a huge disappointment. In his head, Elisha could hear Rav Kadosh laughing and thought, *he knows that there aren't any real ones left*. Elisha's patience was frazzled. The sun was shining at its full strength, and that meant it was time to try the first afternoon services at the Wall again. He ran down the 144 stairs to the Kotel plaza, hoping that he'd have better luck, but the only luck he had was that 'Natan' was still on security duty and there hadn't been any more sonic booms. He scouted the plaza like a trained spy, and felt sure that he had already seen more than half of these Kohanim already. It was another huge waste of time. The fast was really starting to get to him too. He was a lousy faster and already unbearably hungry and thirsty, and it wasn't even two o' clock. It was annoying that he wasn't at home. At least there he could have someone to complain and whine to.

Just the thought of going back up the 144 steps to scout the other halls made Elisha feel exhausted. He did it slowly, which probably was worse, because his head was in the direct sunlight the entire time. Not only that, the stone was giving him heat prostration as it continued to warm up his whole body. By the time he had made it up the stairs, he was so parched he could only swallow with a dry palate. But then, he became momentarily un-obsessed with his fast because *Jonathan Marks* was sitting leisurely on the steps right ahead of him. Elisha recognized him instantly, even though he had never seen him in real life before. He was popularly known to all of Professor Bezalel's students as 'The Other'. That was the name given to him by Professor Bezalel, but that's not the name that appeared under his photo on the many school bulletin boards, where his picture could still clearly be seen as president of his graduating class. Actually, Jonathan, or 'The Other', was one of the only ones who had ever made it to Chamber Seven, which was always a huge deal, because if you were lucky, only *one* person reached *Seven* status each year. There was some kind of process of elimination, and as they all knew, there were only three to date who had *ever* gotten that far. But, Jonathan left. He left Professor Bezalel. He left the Old City. And he left full of hatred. He had become a successful journalist for a big newspaper, and at every opportunity, he would bash their school. He had said that Professor Bezalel suffered from 'Jerusalem Syndrome', or as his mother explained, 'he was mentally challenged'. The bad publicity was no small matter. It had triggered watchful law enforcement eyes and suspicion in general. Interestingly enough, Jonathan, or 'The Other', never exposed in his many articles exactly what took place in the Chambers themselves, which was a huge disappointment for all those uninitiated. Elisha couldn't imagine what he was doing back in the neighborhood, but it didn't matter to Elisha. Jonathan wasn't a Kohen, and certainly 'The Other' wouldn't qualify for his search.

Elisha saw Jonathan taking out a chilled cola from

his pack and then guzzling away at it. That in itself was pretty disrespectful when everyone over the age of 12 or 13 was fasting, and he was a *Seven*. At the moment, in Elisha's parched state, the chilled cola took on the proportions of a mirage. Then 'The Other' spoke to him, and with a "Hey, heads up," tossed him something. Elisha looked at his hands that now had caught a frosty, chilled can of cola. He heard himself automatically say, "Thanks", but wasn't sure that should be the answer. Jonathan surely recognized the school insignia on Elisha's shirt and was probably trying to be disrespectful to him too, but Elisha kept mounting the stairs. Even just holding the chilled can to his face gave him newfound strength, but there was also a chill that radiated through his whole spine, and he was too scared to turn around, feeling with utter certainty that Jonathan Marks was staring at him going up the stairs. He probably wanted to see if Elisha would drink the cola. Elisha quickly turned the corner and headed into the entrance way of the Aish Center, dumping the unopened can as quickly as he could into the garbage.

At least the Kohanim there were super-friendly, but apparently no direct descendants were to be found. Elisha managed to cover five more priestly blessings that afternoon, and his only encouraging thought was that at least he was indoors, but nothing turned up at any of them. He painfully saw the time on his watch. It was 5:00pm. He was torn. Part of him felt that time was flying by too fast, and he needed it to slow down so that he could find the Kohen in time, but as far as his stomach was concerned, time was dragging by way too slowly, and he wanted to eat and drink already. He groaned, thinking he would have to wait another three hours to break his fast. He knew he didn't have to keep fasting. He knew he was being stubbornly weird, but for some reason, he just felt he couldn't break his fast until he had found the Kohen. No, it was that he thought that he'd only be able to find the Kohen if he kept fasting. Actually, the only thing he was thinking about every minute was food.

The last thing anyone was thinking about at Mt. Scopus Hospital was the fast. Rebecca had gone into premature labor after Daniel's unsuccessful surgery. He had started having violent convulsions, and she was pacing the hospital hallways shouting desperately for a nurse, while trying to hold her massive and bouncing pregnant stomach in place. Four doctors had rushed him into intensive care, and their voices and movements rang of urgency as they tried to stabilize him. Rebecca had doubled over in pain instead of following the quickly rolling hospital bed through the swinging doors. Two interns rushed her over to the maternity ward in a wheelchair.

It was a difficult labor because she was fighting it. Rebecca hadn't wanted this baby to be born on the 17th of Tammuz. She had wanted to wait another three weeks for the 9th of Av. Although she still didn't know why. Her only consolation between screams and pushes was that at least the 17th of Tammuz was the second to worst date on the Hebrew calendar.

Ezra was running around in circles, torn between where to direct the focus of his worries, his sister or his brother-in-law. He rushed back and forth like a madman between the maze of hospital wards which were on opposite sides of the expansive complex, and was totally oblivious to the fact that he hadn't eaten for almost 24 hours.

The maternity nurses had mistaken him for the father. They couldn't help smirking at seeing him rushing around so distraught, pale, and perspiring. They had seen more than their fair share of hysterical husbands, but this guy was really up there. The newest midwife on staff gave him the good news.

She announced with a smile, "You can take a deep breath now, Mr. Bezalel. Your wife is fine, and you have a healthy new baby daughter. " She handed him a small swaddled package.

He automatically took the little bundle in his arms. His new niece. He caught his breath and told them, "I'm not the father." He passed the pink bundle back into their surprised faces and excused himself, while rushing back out in the other direction. "I'm the uncle. The father is fighting for his life in intensive care."

Elisha felt that he qualified for one of those survivor shows as he descended for the fourth time. He was so lightheaded, he practically felt like he was flying down the whole way, and would have been happy to eat fish eyes if he didn't know what they were. There was a group of small children sitting on the side steps, and Elisha could see they were eating—dividing up his favorite chocolate bar without a care in the world. He started feeling waves of cold sweat. He was so delirious that the thought crossed his mind to snatch it right out of their hands.

That's when he decided to hang it up. He was just too weak to do anything anymore, and he didn't even know if the anything he was doing was anything at all.

He maneuvered his way through the crowd to reach the Wall itself and just leaned against it. Even in the blazing heat, the stones were cool to the touch. It was time for his newly-concocted last ditch plan. He lowered his head down and took note of the massive stones below him. He could see their chiseled edges and knew they were the ones Herod's builders had put in place—original Second Temple stones. Elisha touched his pouch to them, desperately hoping, in a sick way, for there to be a massive earthquake or a volcanic sonic boom, or *anything* that would let him run back to the garbage and retrieve the can of cola he had thrown out, but instead he felt all of the blood in his body pumping into his brain like a water balloon, and he immediately had to lift his head up before it exploded. Then he heard his brain move. He quickly closed his eyes and thought he saw bright blue lights. He had heard that people saw lights before they fainted, and with his nutrition-starved and dehydrated brain, he realized he had better sit down.

It was 7:01pm, and he only had an hour left, but he knew it was already over. He sat down near the stone wash basin. It was the absolute best he could do. The sun was setting behind the Wall like a pancake on fire, but you couldn't eat it, and everyone else seemed just fine, except for him. He helplessly watched the minutes go by, still too dizzy to get up. So simple, but he couldn't do it.

At 7:05, Jonathan was finished. He had 'received' what he was hunting for and had just spent five hours hanging around to savor it. He couldn't exactly say how he had done it, but he also didn't care to give it a second thought. He looked up at the twilight sky and was ravenous for his own horizon, even though he knew it would require intensive training to get there. There would be no choice except to start from Chamber One and then advance methodically, a chamber at a time, until he was all the way back up to the Seventh. So what . . . he'd cram those seven years of empowerment into three weeks even if it exhausted him to death, as long as he could be ready for the 9th of Av *this year*. It was barely an inconvenience considering what was at stake. He stifled a laugh. The 'eternal' city had opened its gates to him today.

Jonathan continued walking uphill toward the Zion Gate to get to his parked car. He ran his hands over the solid Jerusalem stone walls of Suleiman the Magnificent. They were only solid for now. As he exited through the other side of the arched gateway, he closed his eyes and deeply breathed in the charged air. The city of King David was to his right, and King Hezekiah's secret tunnel was right under his feet. The ancient powerhouses of Solomon, Zedekiah, and Herod were all here, everywhere. He suddenly convulsed, and grabbed a hold of the roof of his car as he uncontrollably threw up his fast-food dinner.

Elisha checked his watch. It was 7:59pm, four minutes left to the end of the fast, and all he wanted to do was to go home.

When he stood up, the pounding in his head actually made noise. On top of being a total failure, he knew his brain was cracking into two. He looked up to the sky to see if three stars had come out signaling the end of the 17th of Tammuz. There was one. It was enough. He quickly lowered his eyes as a thump of lightheadedness made him feel severely nauseous. He started putting one foot in front of the other, but after barely two steps, he simply couldn't move. He had to sit down that second, just for a second, or he instinctively knew that he'd faint. When he did, he was even more sickened to realize that he was in the spot where the usual row of beggars sat. A huge and shabby-looking beggar gave him a disapproving look. Elisha didn't care, and just dropped his head down onto his knees, which gave him a great view of the beggar's filthy and blackened hands. That made him feel like he would throw up right there on the spot, so he tried to move, but the exertion was too much for him, and in his unsteadiness, he felt a terrible pain piercing through his entire body as his arm accidentally brushed against the grotesque black hand. In his panic, he was sure he was having a pre-death convulsion, or maybe contracting beggar disease or even amnesia, until he realized it wasn't coming from his body. It was the *stone* in the pouch attached to his waist. It was pulsating violently and heating up by the second. He quickly removed it, but his hands started to feel on fire, and in an instant he uncontrollably dropped the pouch into the beggar's lap. A blinding light burst in front of the small space between them. Did the beggar see *that*, or was it only in his own brain? All Elisha could think of, with his heart pounding out of control, was that there was a *real Kohen* left. He didn't remember anything after that. He had fainted on the spot.

Aaron Kohen was no weak man. He was homeless and 'freelancing' at the Wall, but he was still worth his weight in lifting heavy loads, better than most men half his age. He'd even been awarded "Employee of the Year" at Mega Movers before he got fired six months before.

Great, thought Aaron, *just my luck, a sick kid to deal with.*

He thought of taking off quickly with whatever crazy and probably very expensive computer toy gadget was in the pouch, but he wasn't really sure the kid had 'given' it to him, and with the Wall looming to his left, he thought better of it. Not only that, he suddenly felt a pain of self-disgust so tight that he thought he was going to be sick too. He was going to do the right thing, and he quickly brought some water from the fountain and sprinkled it over the boy's face.

"Hey kid, wake up now, we've got to get you home. Where do you live?"

Elisha came to, and Aaron couldn't help but notice the large pale blue eyes.

Elisha felt too weak to walk, but before he could get the words out, Aaron had effortlessly lifted him, with one arm around his shoulder, to a standing position with his feet dangling in the air just inches from the ground, and said, "Just lead the way, kiddo."

Elisha found it difficult to speak. His mouth was as dry as sandpaper, but he managed to get out his address. Aaron knew exactly where it was.

"What's your name, kid?" Aaron asked. But it was more to keep the kid conscious than to make conversation.

Even though Elisha's head was splitting in pain, he was feverishly happy and even managed to say. "Elisha

Davidson, and yours?"

"Aaron, Aaron Kohen," said the beggar.

Elisha laughed dryly and hysterically in relief, "I knew it, I knew it."

Aaron was sure this kid would need to go straight to the emergency room tonight. He knew the rap, he'd been there himself. Lucky for Aaron, this would be a quickie; the kid lived on Gates Street, no more than a five-minute walk, although easily about 150 stairs up, but, it was no problem for a man with his experience. Elisha weighed about a half a mini fridge, and Aaron could easily carry at least three of those at one time.

After phoning just about every friend Elisha had ever had, the Davidsons were well into parental phase two—complete panic, and were quickly heading to phase three—utter hysteria, especially because it was the 17th of Tammuz. There was already the bad news of Professor Bezalel's botched surgery which had left him fighting for his life and in a coma.

Where had Elisha disappeared to? And how come *no one* knew where he was? Tamar Davidson's hands were shaking as she started making the dreaded call to the police.

Aaron barely knocked once and the door practically flew open. The Davidson's faces registered instant alarm. What on earth was a sheet-white Elisha doing in the arms of a filthy homeless person?

Aaron at times honestly forgot what he had become, and he suddenly realized just how bad the whole scene looked. He spoke quickly. "Sorry, Sir, Mam, I think the boy must have fasted today and was weak. He fainted by the Wall, and I just wanted to help bring him home."

Both parents exhaled loudly at the same time.

But Elisha's father couldn't shift his stressed-out gears so easily. He glared at Elisha and demanded, "And just *where* were you all day??!! Well, what do you have to say for yourself??!!"

Elisha's mother was already tilting a cup of orange juice straight into Elisha's mouth.

"Didn't I tell you to come right home!!? What does it *mean* to come right home, Elisha??!!" he demanded angrily again.

His mother kept up a barricade between Elisha and his father. "Thank goodness you're okay!" and without taking her eyes off Elisha she asked, "Where's my phone? I want to call Dr. Goldman."

Elisha's father was obviously annoyed. "You can't bother him with *this*!" but then he focused his aggravation back onto Elisha. "Your mother was worried sick about you all day!!"

Tamar Davidson was already calling the unlisted private cellphone number with her free hand. Even Elisha cringed. Dr. Goldman was their next-door neighbor, Joseph's dad, but even he knew she shouldn't be calling the chief of surgery. He could also tell by her increasingly calm 'Okays' and 'thank you's' that he was going to be fine. It didn't matter; all that really mattered to Elisha at that moment was the juice. It was the best Elisha had ever tasted, and with each sip he could feel his whole body being watered like a thirsty plant.

Aaron stood uncomfortably at the door and then turned around to leave. Elisha's father quickly remembered his manners and invited the homeless man into the house. He brought him firmly over to the dinner table, which was all laid out to break the fast. Aaron couldn't say no. He had been running on an empty stomach well before the 17th of Tammuz had started, and it wasn't like he had somewhere to go. Suddenly, all the attention on the food abruptly turned towards Elisha's mother's call.

"That's fantastic news!! Thank goodness!!" She looked at them all triumphantly. "You wouldn't believe it. Dr. Goldman told me that Professor Bezalel just made it through, barely ten minutes ago. He's out of the coma!! Still with amnesia though . . . and not only that," she smiled from ear to ear, "they have a new daughter. Mother and baby are doing just fine!" The whole household now generated a feel-good atmosphere, where only minutes before it was dark and morose.

Orange juice was a wonder drug for Elisha, and so was the plate of food his mother was feeding him in small portions in his bed according to the doctor's instructions. But the minute she left him he could hear both of his parents' voices outside of his room, although they were fading fast as they walked down the hallway.

"You not only abandoned him, *you* told him to fast didn't you, DIDN'T YOU?" his mother demanded.

"I told him until 1:00pm," his father answered sheepishly.

"Well, you should have been *clear*."

"I was *100% clear*."

Elisha rarely felt bad for this father, but this was one of those rare moments. Mom was definitely going to lace into him, but nothing could have changed Elisha's good mood. He lay comfortably under his covers reliving the entire day. Who would have thought that the Kohen of

Light would be a homeless person? And what's he going to do with the stone, Elisha wondered. Does he have the other 11 to make a complete set? He was also glad that he was spared knowing about Professor Bezalel's near encounter with death until it was all okay again.

He could hear the voices of the adults at the dinner table. Strange—they sounded really lively and engaged in happy conversation like they were old friends. Elisha was also dying to speak to Aaron Kohen to get some answers. His thoughts were making him restless, but he honestly did feel too weak to get out of bed. Besides, his mother would never allow it, and she was coming in every ten minutes to check on him. It took about an hour for the adult conversation to die out. Funny, but his own conversation with Rav Kadosh seemed like it was a month ago already, even though he hadn't forgotten a single word, and that he had said his mother was special. He, of course, thought so too. He loved her with his whole heart, but she was just a regular mom, wasn't she? He also remembered the ridiculous stuff that he hadn't wanted to remember. After all, he would have known if he had almost died when he was little. He did have a scar on his arm from when he fell in the park and landed on a piece of broken glass when he was three, but it wasn't shaped like a lightning bolt, and as far as he knew, it wasn't life threatening either. He made a small note in his mind that even though Rav Kadosh was a Mekubal, he didn't know *everything*, and it did leave that small open space called doubt.

Aaron just couldn't refuse this kind family's invitation to sleep in a real bed for the night. They insisted. It was the least they could do for someone who had saved their son, and well, they actually didn't have to insist at all. He was also much honored, because he had known Mrs. Davidson's grandfather, but he was afraid to tell them how. Now he knew why those blue eyes had looked so hauntingly familiar.

Sitting on the bed of the comfortable room, Aaron said to himself, 'Now, I could get used to this.' Without changing into the pajamas that he didn't own, he had stretched out on the soft clean-smelling bed, when he remembered the boy's pouch. He reached over and opened it. After looking inside it, he tried his best to stay calm. He zipped it closed and assured himself, *OK, now you see it and now it's gone.* Aaron lay back in the bed thoroughly disgusted with himself. It was *those* hallucinations again! Those same ones that had gotten him fired. The same ones that convinced all the doctors that he was crazy. The craziness was coming back! He grabbed the pillow and held it tight over his face. He would have liked to smother himself to death at that very moment. Then he remembered he was supposed to breathe in and out calmly. That's how they told him to do it, and that's what he was going to do. The otherworldly disco lights were going to stay IN the bag and not in his mind. It was easy this time, and Aaron Kohen quickly fell asleep in the comfortable surroundings.

Mother and baby were actually not doing fine. Rebecca was sobbing quietly to herself under the dim nightlight that hung over her hospital bed. Her birth experience had rated right up there with a near death experience—Daniel's. She closed her eyes to try and regain some composure. But then she found herself obsessing about the name again. He hadn't even told her what the name should be! How could he have forgotten to do something so important before he went blank? Names were *everything* to him. How could he have done this!! She opened up her eyes to stop her rising anger. She had a view of the nurses' station from her bed and could see that the head nurse from Daniel's unit was there too. *You couldn't get rid of that horrendous woman. She was everywhere.* She was even inquiring about her. She felt her throat catch while her whole body turned rigid. She couldn't stand to hear any more bad news. *It would be cruel and unusual punishment. I just gave birth. Leave me alone. I don't want to know anything.*

The stern and matronly woman approached her bedside. "I came to tell you that he's alright now. All vital signs are stable."

She took Rebecca's hand and held it stiffly. Rebecca felt that she was holding on for life. She swallowed as her whole body released itself from a high pressure vacuum, and watched as the nurse's pristine and soft-creped shoes headed toward the well-lit hallway. She could breathe now. She breathed in again. At least things were back to bad and not worse. She felt the tension melting out of her body. She stared at her surroundings. Whether she wanted to or not, she'd be forced to rest here for the next three days. It suddenly occurred to her that she hadn't had this much time for herself in weeks. She had been juggling, struggling, and overstretching herself since the accident. It would finally give her time to hear herself think. The kids were in the good hands of her sister-in-law, and she was going to be content and totally fine with having the competent nurses look after her tiny, new,

no-named baby. She absolutely was *not* going to squan-
der this precious time with more of the same constant,
sickening migraine-producing worrying about Daniel.
There were lots of things she needed to think about. One
of them was a name, and she kept drawing blanks, as if
she couldn't even think up a name for her own daughter
without Daniel. That bothered her. Didn't she have her
own favorite name?

But she couldn't think, because her mind was instantly accosted by an all too familiar smell. Rebecca
didn't even have to open her eyes to know that Great
Aunt Esther had walked into the ward. Her minty moth-
ball scent always preceded her anywhere. Rebecca was
instantly infuriated at how her first attempt at quiet time
was about to be totally obliterated. She heard a familiar
echo in her head. *This is cruel and unusual punishment.
How could the nurses be so negligent to let in a visitor
now? I just gave birth. Leave me alone!* She could hear
Great Aunt Esther's heavy shuffling footsteps along with
the rustling sound of polyester getting closer, and it was
a soundtrack made for a horror show.

Aunt Esther moved the partitioned curtains all the
way to the side and immediately brought her finger to her
lips with a "SHHhhh . . . ." And then in a conspiratorial
hush she said, "I had to tell zhem I vaz your grandmozzer
or zhey vouldn't let me in to zee you. Can you imagine?
And zhat's *after* I told zhem zhat I'm here on an urgent
family matter zhat couldn't vait."

Rebecca tried to raise herself higher up now. She
couldn't imagine what it could be.

Great Aunt Esther plopped down weightily in the
comfortable visitor's recliner chair which was definitely
too low for her, and Rebecca could see that her ortho-

pedic stockings were like tourniquets at the top of her calves. She leaned far enough forward to be able to pat Rebecca's hand.

"Mazal Tov, dear," she said, and then breathed in and out heavily with the weight of her important mission. "Vell, you know me, and I vouldn't have come all zhe vay out here if it vasn't sumtink important, and believe me," she waved her hand dramatically, "after a veek and a half of havink to subztitute for your huzband for zhose terriblly vild and *chutzbadik* boys, I'm *still* not back to myself. And vhat vit my high blood pressure, heart problemz and diabeedeez, you can imagine zhat I only came out because it'z sumtink urgent too!"

"What is it?" Rebecca asked with concern, but she didn't have enough energy to start forcing it out of her.

"I told you already, a family matter of zhe highest importance, and I had to make sure to come before it vaz too late. I hope it'z not already *too* late."

"Too late for *what*?"

"Zhe name, of course!! I vanted to remind you zhat vee still don't have anyone in zhe family named after my beloved sizter, Faygalah Blooma. Vhat a shame, izn't it?"

Rebecca couldn't help cringing, but turned it into a painful smile.

Great Aunt Esther looked at Rebecca. "Vhat'z zhe matter dear? You look a little pale," she said as she patted her hand again, "and zince you're my favorite grandnieze and you bear zhe name of your very own grandmozzer—I'm sure you know vhat zhe right ting to do iz."

Rebecca just stared at the floor. She couldn't believe what she was dealing with, and that's when she also noticed a bag and remembered that Great Aunt Esther always brought homemade out-of-this-world apple strudel when she made a hospital visit. Rebecca wished she would just leave it there and go away quickly, but life wasn't like that. There was no free strudel.

Great Aunt Esther waited for any sign of agreement from Rebecca, but when there wasn't any, she continued, "And just betveen us, your husband vazn't very cooperative vit all zhe ozher namez I vanted and I never said a vord. But, since he doezn't remember his own name . . . ," Great Aunt Esther thankfully stopped herself. She sighed loudly and put her hand on her heart. "Oy, vhat a poor ting. You know I just came frum seeink him, but zhey vouldn't let me go in. I had to look from zhe door."

"He's not doing very well today," Rebecca explained. She didn't have the heart to tell the truth, that Daniel was pronounced clinically dead today for three minutes and six seconds.

The Avarshina had known that and it is why it came, but Great Aunt Esther shook her head and tisked, "Vell, I hope it'z not too seriouz." She leaned in close towards Rebecca's face and said quietly, "I don't like to even say such tingz, but I saw prisonerz in Aushsvitz zhat looked healtier." She patted Rebecca's hand and said, "Vell, it vazn't like he ever had a goot appetite. But don't feel too bad about it, dear, your grandmozzer and mozzer, *may zhey rest in peace*, vere terrible cookz and I luved zhem vit my whole heart." She patted Rebecca's hands again. "It's not your fault, dear. You couldn't be expected to learn a ting from eider vone in zhe kitchen."

Rebecca could barely stand this friendly family visit for a nanosecond longer. She turned her face to the end table. *Over. Let it be over. Please. Fast.*

Great Aunt Esther got the message. "I better let you get some rezt and bezidez, I have a very buzy schedule of people to vizit here zhis evening."

Great. Just don't list them, and don't tell me any of their ailments. Relieved, Rebecca watched as she gathered her things and looked at her watch, which seemed to be cutting off all of her circulation. She left the bag of strudel on the rollable hospital end table and turned to Rebecca again, adjusting her scuba diving goggles.

"Now remember, dear, it'z *Faygalah Blooma*," she said, and before leaving the curtained partition, she pronounced it again, slower, and the accent was even worse.

Rebecca's head was throbbing. Hearing *that* name had the effect of wiping out any normal name she had ever known. She shuddered. What had Dr. Allon told her in that distant and cold voice . . . that she should prepare herself, that she should make arrangements . . . Why couldn't she even think of one? Wasn't there even *one*? She searched her mind frantically. There wasn't. She swallowed hard. He wasn't just the *Arranger of Letters*. He had managed to rearrange her whole life! People had warned her that she should think twice before spending her life with a crazed genius. They told her that he'd end up driving her crazy with all that passionate, genius-driven intensity. They were married for fifteen years already, and she could attest to the fact that they were right. People were always saying how Daniel was *so* 'gifted'. They couldn't even fathom what the word meant in his case. Only she knew. She reached for the bag of strudel and smiled when she saw there were two. That was fun. She probably got Daniel's too. There was also a pink note in the bag; it was addressed to the parents of Elisha Davidson. Who was that?

After about an hour, she remembered that she did have a favorite name. She always loved the name Alicia.

She thought about the Hebrew equivalent, which would be Elisha. That was a boy's name. Too bad. Daniel wasn't there to arrange the letters of this name. Well, that had been her favorite name. She called for the nurses. She wanted to see Alicia.

CHAPTER 6

The Kohen of Light

With the bright rays of late morning sun, Elisha was up and felt that he had regained all his strength. So what if Chamber One summer camp was cancelled, he was having his own better version. The events of the previous day were buzzing like crazy in his mind. He went to wash up and was surprised to hear a strange voice in the house. He quickly realized that the beggar, or Priest of Light, must have stayed overnight! Elisha quickened his pace, he *had* to speak to him before he left. Just as he reached the kitchen, there was a knock on the front door. Elisha shouted out, "I'll get it."

Elisha was deeply annoyed to see that it was Josh again. It wasn't that he didn't like his best friend; it's just that it was really bad timing, *again*. Josh came right in and quickly noticed the beggar, and looked surprised.

"Hi, Uncle Aaron, what are you doing here?"

"Hey, buddy," was the response.

Elisha was more surprised than Josh. The reality of the words hit him hard—Uncle Aaron? Well, that meant, what, that all of yesterday's search could have been as easy as getting together with his best friend!!? Elisha's admiration for Josh instantly shot up. Josh must be a real Kohen too . . . but then how could he let his uncle be a beggar on the street? And *wait* a minute, Elisha had definitely seen Josh's father—*nothing* had happened. Something was off. It wasn't just finding a real Kohen, there had to be something about the 'light' part which made Aaron special. He reminded himself that Rav Kadosh didn't know *everything*.

Tamar Davidson came on the scene and quickly inspected Elisha. She was happy with what she saw. "Well, gentlemen, how about a late breakfast?"

They were all quick to the table. Aaron sized up the boy he had 'saved' the night before. He looked pretty healthy and normal this morning. Elisha was sizing up the beggar who must have showered and shaved, and it was amazing how entirely different he looked now. Despite his large size, he had very pleasant features. He even looked like a rugged action hero from the movies. Even with everyone around, Elisha was sure that he'd exchange some sort of *knowing* and secretive look with him, but he didn't.

Mrs. Davidson was happy to announce, "Aaron is going to be staying with us for a while, just until he gets settled in with his new job at Dad's library."

Elisha thought he couldn't have planned a better conspiracy himself. He'd now have lots of time to talk to the Kohen of Light privately. Josh was genuinely happy.

"That's great, Uncle Aaron, what are you going to be doing?" he asked.

"Just the usual shleppin', kiddo," Aaron replied.

Elisha's mother set three different boxes of cereal on the table and brightly added, "And your father came up with another good idea last night too, for you Elisha, now that the Chambers are cancelled."

That could only be trouble, thought Elisha, and he quickly focused all his attention onto the back of the cereal box.

"Well, your father thought that since you'll have so much free time, you could use some of it to help out Aaron by teaching him how to use a computer."

Elisha relaxed, although he could hardly believe that there was anyone left on the planet who didn't know how to use one.

"No, it's all right, I'm sure he's got much better things to do than to teach an old dog new tricks."

Mrs. Davidson and Elisha spoke up at the same time, but it was Elisha's voice that held.

"I can teach you," he said sincerely, and his mother's face was all approvals.

"You could have asked me," Josh added. "I'd teach you, at night if you want, because I'm in soccer camp during the day."

Aaron looked at Elisha again. "Well then, Elisha is stuck with me, but don't you worry, I promise to be a good student," and he winked.

Tamar Davidson carefully surveyed Elisha again. He really did look fine. She was relieved that she could get to work and was anxious to go. She pointed the boys in the direction of Elisha's room right after they had finished eating and was off with a "Have fun."

Elisha was reluctant. Josh hadn't seen the inside of his room since the stone was brought in. He wondered how long it would take for him to notice it. He really wanted to confide in Josh, and maybe he should. After all, he was the Kohen of Light's nephew.

"Cool stone." Josh's reaction was quick and then disinterested.

But Elisha's was quite the opposite. Josh *didn't* reflect in the mirror stone. There was only a black shadow where his reflection should be. Josh clearly didn't notice anything strange, because he was arranging his baseball cap facing the stone. Elisha felt spooked, and it definitely made him think twice about opening up to Josh. It was actually Josh who wanted to confide something "else" to Elisha.

"I don't want to have this sound like I'm saying something bad about someone, but uh, like your father should know. I mean I hope someone lets him know, because like everyone else does, and I bet he does anyways, so just so *you* know, my uncle is completely crazy, and I mean like a major wacko. So, what's he doing in your house?"

Elisha just stared at Josh. Josh was honestly telling him that he had just given the find of the millennium to a wacko. "What do you mean?" he asked naively trying not to give away the total flipped-out disappointment in his voice.

"I mean he's, well, my parents say he's traumatized. You know. I told you about my cousins that were killed in that terrorist explosion, well that's *that* uncle."

Elisha, of course, had heard about *that* story. Everyone knew about it, but no one had ever met *that* side of the family.

"Our whole family has been trying to deal with him for years, and he never lets us help him or anything, so I'm glad that he's letting your father help him, however long that lasts," he added sarcastically. "He went totally crazy after it and that's all there is to it."

Elisha ventured carefully, "So, what makes him crazy? I mean he seems okay."

"Oh. I don't know. He sees stuff, hallucinations and

junk like that. I mean he's okay one minute and then . . . he's just not. But don't worry, he's completely harmless."

Elisha's heart sank like a rock. *Hello to wacko number two*, he thought.

Time passed slowly taking turns on Flightpilot with Josh, especially because Elisha was still eager to have some private time with 'Uncle Wacko'. At noon, and at long last, Josh went home for lunch.

Elisha knocked softly at the guest room door and heard, "Door's open." He didn't really know where to start, but he looked deeply into Aaron's eyes for some hint of unspoken understanding, or even better, one of Rav Kadosh's quick-winded lectures. But Aaron just looked kindly at Elisha and asked, "What can I do you for?"

Elisha cautiously asked, "What are you going to do with the stone?"

Aaron looked straight at him and asked, "What stone?"

Elisha was confused. "What? You didn't even take it out and look at it?"

"You mean whatever is in that pouch of yours?"

Aaron reached for his shoes. Elisha noticed they were in horrible condition.

"What's in it anyways, some kind of new-fangled game? It scared me half to death last night when it nearly blinded me." Aaron reached for a bottle of black shoe polish. "What was that, some kind of joke?" Aaron wasn't really asking, he was just hoping that that's what it was.

Elisha was puzzled. "No. It's a special stone. A *Cho* . . . ." He shook his head and asked, "You didn't even see what it was?"

Aaron was now busy polishing his shoes. Elisha couldn't understand why the Kohen of Light wasn't even reacting to him. He tried again. "You didn't understand it was something special? Didn't you see all those strange lights that came out last night when I gave it to you?"

It was the wrong question and some sort of bad trigger. Aaron started breaking out in a cold sweat. "Hey listen. If you wanna be crazy, then go ahead, but I'll have nothin' to do with yah. I'm not crazy, thank you. You be the crazy one, okay? I'll have no part of it. No part of it *whatsoever*."

Elisha instantly felt utterly lost, but had to try again. "But, aren't you the Kohen of Light?'

That did it. Aaron's eyes were shifting and twitching at the same time. He grabbed a hold of Elisha's arm.

"You saw it too, didn't you? The light. Didn't you! Tell me, didn't you!!"

His arm started shaking Elisha's in total desperation. Elisha felt so confused. It wasn't at all how he thought things would turn out, and even though he didn't know why, he found the same irritating question coming out of his mouth again: "But, aren't you the Kohen of Light??!!"

With that, Aaron's whole body stiffened like a statue. Only his eyes moved as they stared up at the ceiling. Then he looked like he was talking to someone else.

"Yeah, *sure*, I'm the *crazy* man who sees lights." He let out an abrupt laugh. "But *no* one ever called me *the Kohen of Light* before—'Victim of Terror' sure, but yup, that's me, the crazy guy named Kohen who sees lights. Yup, ringin' in my ears, flashes of lights."

He went back to polishing his shoes furiously in quick sharp movements. "Lights? Now you see 'em and now you don't. They said they would disappear. Yup, just disappear, just like that. And then kids even start callin' you the *Kohen of Light*! " A high-pitched staccato laugh left his mouth, and then he started mumbling something softly, "Couldn't disappoint them and tell them I was born seeing lights . . . and the biggest light?" He closed his eyes tight and screamed, "*NO.*"

Elisha had never seen an adult falling to pieces like this, especially not such a strong looking man. It was one of the most pathetic things he had ever seen in his life. He moved backwards to the door as quickly as possible and quietly let himself out. Aaron needed privacy.

Elisha needed information, and he needed it fast. Now he wished Josh hadn't gone home so quickly. He walked out his front door. He was going to get answers.

Dr. Brody put his hand gently on Jonathan's shoulder. "Two detectives will be here in about another 20 minutes."

Jonathan faked a wince.

Dr. Brody breathed in. "You know, you don't have to do this."

Jonathan stiffened with feigned determination. "Of course I do. Come on, don't you understand? These people are sick! And the only way I'm going to get back my memory or to get anyone else to believe me is by going through with this." He truly hoped that Dr. Brody was buying into his 'heartfelt' performance.

Jonathan was so adamant that Dr. Brody felt confident it was the right decision. He softly added with a calm and resigned tone, "Okay, then let's get started."

"Wait," Jonathan added. "Don't let them in through the door until you have me well into it."

"Of course," Dr. Brody answered.

Jonathan stretched his arms over his head and sat himself down on the sofa. "And, let's give them their money's worth. Regress me to the Seventh Chamber, 17th of Tammuz, four years ago."

Dr. Brody hesitated. "But, but we're only up to Chamber Four."

Jonathan was smiling smugly. "I guarantee you, Dr. Brody, they only get better."

Against his better judgment, Dr. Brody proceeded to put Jonathan into a hypnotic state on his requested date. "Where are you now?" he asked.

"I'm in the Foundation Vault and it's extremely dark."

"Can you tell me who is with you?"

"The Arranger of Letters is with me."

Dr. Brody stopped his establishing questions. That was a name that he had never heard of before. He jotted it down and waited another ten minutes for the 'short version' chanting to be over. He then went quietly into his reception room where the two detectives were already waiting and invited them into his office.

"You can come in now."

They jumped up noisily, so Dr. Brody quickly set down some ground rules.

"Please, I must insist that you observe without making any noise whatsoever."

The two detectives followed him in and sat down as quietly as possible, although it was clear by their expressions that they thought this was a total waste of their time.

Jonathan was standing in the center of the room with his eyes tightly shut. He started to move his mouth intensely without any words coming out. It was like he was chanting, but lost his voice. Dr. Brody furrowed his lips. Jonathan looked quite comical, and one of the detectives stifled a laugh with a cough. Dr. Brody quickly repeated his establishing question.

"Jonathan, can you describe where you are standing?"

"I'm in a subterranean chamber several feet under the Temple Mount."

That sentence was enough to peak the detectives' attention. One was now leaning forward to catch every word, while the other started jotting down notes.

"And who are you with?"

"I've left my class now and I'm alone with my teacher, the Arranger of Letters. He's speaking fire."

Dr. Brody realized that he would need to establish a name, so he tried again, "And what is your teacher's *real* name?"

Jonathan answered clearly and firmly, "The Arranger of Letters is his *real* name."

Dr. Brody left off that questioning and tried to make progress elsewhere. "And what is he teaching you?"

Jonathan's face contorted as he deeply voiced, *"Abracadabra, abracadabra."*

Both detectives burst out laughing at once. Jonathan instantly fell out of his hypnotic trance, while Dr. Brody became flustered. The tall detective didn't bother being polite.

"Sorry, Doc, but what are you running here, a comedy show?"

The detective, who was a head shorter than him, snorted, "This guy watched too many cartoons when he was a kid."

They snickered in unison again, and the minute they walked out to the reception room, they were cracking up laughing.

Dr. Brody was quick to shut his door, but not quick enough to close out a loud, raucous, "What a joke!"

Jonathan was outraged and desperate at the same time. "What was so funny! What did I say that was SO funny?"

Dr. Brody was obviously embarrassed for him, but was obliged to repeat it. "I'm sorry, Jonathan, but you were unfortunately very clearly saying . . . , um . . . *abracadabra*." Dr. Brody shook his head with a knowing sadness that clearly said Jonathan had made a complete fool of himself.

Jonathan was extremely upset and thrilled at the same time, except when he turned to face Dr. Brody. Then he stared squarely and incredulously at him with total contempt. "Are you really *so* ignorant, *Doctor* Brody??"

Dr. Brody stared back with a look of blank confusion.

"Take notes on this one, Doctor. *Abracadabra* is Aramaic, but even if you're clueless about the language of the Talmud—look at the words. It's the same Hebrew alphabet, and *these* words happen to be exactly the same." Jonathan grabbed a notebook off Dr. Brody's desk and was writing and speaking at the same time. "*Abra*—I will create. *Cadabra*—as I speak."

Dr. Brody definitely hesitated for a moment. Funny, that *is* what it meant. He wondered why he had never recognized the words before, probably because they were joined together. It was a nice little factoid to add to his collection. "Cute," he responded, once he 'got' it.

Jonathan was disgusted. "Cute??" It's one of the strongest *practical* Kabbalah phrases there is!"

Dr. Brody was getting sick of Jonathan's intellectual

bullying. "Yes, but admittedly, the only time you hear it is from cartoon characters or lame buffoons pretending to perform magic," he answered in disgust.

Jonathan ignored the tone of his voice and answered academically, "That would be an interesting research project . . . figuring out how one of the most powerful Kabbalah incantations turned into popular Disney." But he let go of that train of thought, and he sat back on Dr. Brody's comfortable sofa. Now he was smiling with a deep and dark satisfaction.

"I never knew that I had mastered it!"

Josh was surprised to see Elisha at his house so quickly.

"Is everything ok?" he asked.

"Yeah, I just . . . I wanted to understand more about your uncle."

Elisha suddenly realized that he probably sounded very nosey and quickly tried to explain himself. "I mean, I want to help him out and all, now that he'll be staying with us for a while."

Josh motioned Elisha to follow him, and he had a look of secrecy about him. They went into his father's study, where Josh stood on a chair and pulled down a photo album scrapbook that was hidden behind several volumes of books on the very top shelf.

"It's all in here," he said seriously, as he started flipping through the pages.

The album was full of newspaper clippings and photos.

"Here, read this one first," Josh said as he handed

Elisha a slightly worn-looking article. "I was only five years old when this whole thing happened, so I don't remember any of it."

The article was long, but Elisha started reading.

It was a suicide bombing. It had taken place in the middle of the day on a heavily traveled intercity route. Seven dead, 25 seriously wounded. Most were kids and teenagers coming back from school. He read on. Josh's uncle was the undisputed hero of the massacre. He had caught sight of the suicide bomber seconds before it happened, and had quickly and single-handedly moved six children and a pregnant woman out of harm's way, while hurling the suicide bomber to the far end of the bus.

"Wow! How did he do that all at once?"

Josh knew what Elisha was asking about. He said proudly, "Are you kidding? I think my uncle is the strongest man on earth!"

Elisha nodded in agreement.

The suicide bomber detonated himself at the back end of the bus, which dramatically minimized the casualties. Had he stayed in the center of it, there wouldn't have been a single survivor. The article went on to the terrible, tragic end. Aaron's own two sons, aged 15 and 17, had run after their father and ended up being in the back blast. Nothing was even left of their bodies. As for Aaron, the force of the explosion had propelled his body out of the bus, and in one of those inexplicable disaster miracles, he had survived it with no real injuries.

No wonder he's such a mess, thought Elisha. What could he or anyone ever do to help him? There were more articles and photos, but most of them just repeated the same information. Just as Elisha was about to close the scrapbook, a large full-color photo caught his eye.

Aaron was standing with his head lowered and his eyes shut tight, as he hugged a strange triangle-shaped metal object to his chest.

"Did he get an award or something?"

Josh checked to see what Elisha was looking at.

"Oh, no, that's one of the weird parts. They had been shopping in town. My cousin Itamar was holding a silver tray, and in the blast, it melted down and reformed itself into that weird-looking thing—whatever it is. At least that's what *he* says. I've actually seen it a couple of times. It's the only thing that my uncle ever saved. He probably still has it. Says it's all he has left in the world."

"Where's your Aunt?"

"Oh, she died a long time ago, even before I was born."

"So your uncle is all alone in the world?"

"*No*, we're here. It's just that my father has done everything in the world to try and help him, but nothing's ever worked. *Nothing!*"

Elisha left with a heavy and depressed feeling. No wonder Aaron was on the street. It's not like he had anyone to go home to. He knew people could lose their minds from something like that. He wished he had known him *before*, because now, well, Aaron wasn't anything like how he had imagined someone who would be called the 'Kohen of Light'.

Elisha entered quietly through the front door of his house. His parents wouldn't be back home yet, and that left just him and crazy Aaron in the house. He didn't really want to see him. Part of him was even afraid of the man. But it was too late. Aaron was in the kitchen, sitting at the table, writing out a note, and he had noticed Elisha come in. Elisha felt, at the very least, he should make polite conversation.

"What are you writing?"

Aaron quickly answered, "I'm leavin', and I just wanted to write a nice thank-you letter to your mom and dad," he said focusing on the note, and then added without looking away from it, "and I'm sorry for what I did to yah."

Elisha's whole body tensed. He was sure Aaron was leaving because of him. He sat straight down across from Aaron and started all out begging himself. "Please don't leave. I promise I won't bother you again. I'm sorry if I said something to make you want to leave."

Aaron looked at Elisha's young face. *Kids!* he thought, *they're just so naïve.* This Elisha was a nice kid too. It wasn't his fault that he brought back all of his crazy visions. "I'll be fine, and it's got nothin' to do with you!"

What a lie! Elisha suddenly felt desperate, but had no idea what to say. How could he try and make Aaron stay, and did he even want him to?

Aaron saw that Elisha was biting his lower lip, and the kid's large pale blue eyes were begging him not to leave, but he didn't have the sophistication to open his mouth. If there's one thing that Aaron Kohen couldn't stand, it was a kid's pleading face. It was his kids every time. His boys needed help. This boy needed something from him, but there was *nothing* left in him to help anyone, not anymore. The silence between them was getting heavier by the second. *Time for a distraction*, thought Aaron. He always had his conversation piece quick at hand. Kids always liked seeing it.

"Hey, before I go, you wanna see somethin' that you've never seen before?" Aaron asked, as he dug under his shirt and pulled out a tarnished flat silver triangle with a rectangular hole in the middle.

Elisha stopped biting his lip and went over to look at it. When he got close, he could see that it was a blob-by-shaped triangle, and there were also weird markings on each side.

Aaron asked, "Well, guess what it is?"

Elisha really wanted to say a *melted down silver tray*. Instead, he politely put out his hands and Aaron passed it over. But when Elisha took it, he dropped it by accident and the thing actually cracked in half on the tiled floor! Elisha didn't know what to do with himself. He had just ruined the *only* thing Aaron had left in his life. He couldn't even bare to look at Aaron's face, and hastily picked up both pieces and pitifully tried to reattach them. The minute he did, a cocoon of multi-colored light, a perfectly outlined rainbow, enveloped his whole body. He was in a rainbow or he was a rainbow. He was mesmerized by himself, and yet at the same time, he was sure that this would be enough to send Aaron running out the door, or maybe even shaking him to death this time.

Aaron wasn't blinking even for a second, and yet his face suddenly seemed painfully happy, if that was at all possible. There was even a sad smile on his face when their eyes locked. It made Elisha feel, for the first time in his life, like he was about to understand some great secret, a sad secret, but it was one he didn't get to know. In the next split second, Aaron grabbed Elisha and threw him up into the air. The pieces disconnected with the force and the rainbow disappeared, but Aaron's whole personality had suddenly 'switched on'.

"Elisha, this is the *best* thing that's happened to me in five years!!" With Elisha in his arms, he ran over to the kitchen table and ripped up the note, and with another huge swing up and down, he lowered Elisha to the floor.

Elisha passed the two broken pieces back to Aaron with a shamefaced, "I'm really sorry."

Aaron backed away. "What?! Are you kiddin'? This is yours! I've been waitin' to give it to *you* for five years.

With that, Aaron went dancing toward the door and out onto the street, truly looking like a bonafide idiot. All he could think to himself was that his life was about to change, but he could never tell a living soul the reason why. He smiled inanely to himself. People were *wrong* about rainbows. They always saw them through rose-tinted, smiley-faced glasses. Sure, they were pretty—pretty deadly. They were a colorful sign and all, but only *after*. That is *after* the entire world was practically wiped out. You needed to know how to read the road signs, and Aaron had just gotten his. He'd never thought there'd ever be an *after*. It had been five long years since his world had been completely wiped out. He hadn't had a single sign that it was ever gonna get better, but the road sign he had just seen was as good as if it had been lit up in Las Vegas neon. Those large, clear blue eyes had told him what to look for. *No*, they had *promised* him . . . but only if he *let go*. That was the catch, only if he could *let go*. He had never mentioned that the blue eyes also belonged to his great-grandson.

Elisha watched Aaron dance down the street, feeling horribly embarrassed for him. There was no doubt about it, Aaron Kohen was crazy, but Elisha knew he wasn't far off himself, and hey, having an accomplice in craziness was certainly better than going at it alone.

The silver triangle was really otherworldly, and now it rested in his hands. Elisha happily went into his room to examine the silvery thing closely and in private. It was strangely ugly, yet hauntingly beautiful. Maybe it wasn't a bad trade after all, a Choshen stone for a whatever-you-call-it rainbow maker. There certainly wasn't one of these in any of Professor Bezalel's textbooks. He wondered how he could fix it. It probably needed to be welded back together, but Elisha did a quick fix with gaffer's tape in the meantime. He was pleased to see that his skills had done the trick. A faint rainbow had come back, and he started waving the silver piece in all different directions, but the rainbow was going on and off all the time. It was like a faulty battery was making it turn on and off. It took him five more minutes to realize what should have been obvious from the start. The closer the silvery thing was to the mirror stone, the more intense the rainbow. It was like it was being powered by the stone: the closer, the better. It was amazing, until he had gotten so close the two could make contact . . . but they didn't make contact. *It was gone.* It wasn't gone, it was his hand! Holding the metal triangle, his hand had gone *through* the rock! He put his hand in and out several times. The mirror stone was no longer solid. How far should he push it? He tried up to his shoulder, everything went inside. He tried his foot, it went inside too. He took his hand out again and put down the metal triangle. The mirror was rock solid again. Did he dare put his head through? Did he dare walk into the stone?? He put his hand through again as far as it would go. He caught a glimpse of a shadow at the entrance of his room. Elisha's body almost jolted to death. It was Aaron watching from the door. He was staring at Elisha. All the while, his brain kept repeating a well-worn mantra: *Let go. Let go. Let go. I've got to let go . . . of whatever sanity I have left. It's not much anyways. Just let it go.*

Elisha's 'caught in the act' face suddenly came into focus, and Aaron said, "I don't think you should be doin' this by yourself." Aaron sighed at the absurdity of his own words. He had just said them as normally as catching a kid with a box of matches or a firecracker. It even sounded as if he had just offered some kind of parental supervision. *Hey, you know you should have Uncle Aaron around when you want to disintegrate parts of your body through a solid rock.* Aaron shifted his stare to the mirror stone and made a firm decision. *Neon or not*, he had done a good enough job of letting go for a month. He turned on his heels to leave the room and then stopped short with a major guilt seizure. He didn't need *this* on his head too.

"*Stop.* OK? Just *stop*! The only adventure you're gonna get out of that thing is a one-way ticket to an insane asylum."

"But, but *you're* the one who gave it to me."

"Right," Aaron said and then hesitated. He took a deep breath, realizing it was going to take a lot more. *How could he get 'Pandora' kid to drop it?* He suddenly became overwhelmed with anxiety and frustration. "Right. I just forgot to tell you that we're ALL done now. You found me, I found you. We traded . . . whatchamacallits . . . and now . . . well, it's over. Finito, as in the END. You did a great job back there. Thanks for helpin' me saaaave the world. *Game's over.* We won. YAY!"

A nasty cynicism hung in the air like toxic waste. Elisha fixed his gaze on the triangle while Aaron let out a long sigh. "OK. It's just that. I mean, you don't get . . . Here's the thing. *Do you have any idea what you were doin' just now?*"

"No," Elisha admitted, and then desperately asked,

"but you do, don't YOU??"

"Nope. Not a clue."

They both sat in silence staring at the floor. After a minute, Aaron got up to leave. He had found his ace, even though he felt like an outright imbecile using it. "Look. I'm not called the '*The Kohen of Light*' for nothin'. And I . . . um . . . command you never to mess around with that thing yourself." Aaron inwardly cringed and then dashed out of the room.

Elisha didn't think he should be doing it by himself either. He desperately wanted to see Rav Kadosh before ever trying it again. The whole thing had freaked him out too, even more than '*Captain* Kohen' realized. He covered the mirror stone while double-checking that his arm was still attached to his body. He smoothed the tape over the crack in the triangle. Obviously, it wasn't the only thing that was broken. He did have to admit that he hadn't been given any other instructions except to *find the Kohen of Light*—and there was nothing in the message about what condition he'd find him in. Maybe it was 'mission accomplished'. Elisha carefully wrapped the triangle up into an old sweater. He tossed the tiny bundle onto the highest shelf of his closet, and let out a hollow and toneless, "Yay."

Principal Ezra Oholiov was sitting quietly in his office. The dim light of his desk lamp barely illuminated the twelve neat stacks of varying height that completely covered the surface of his large desk. An empty school at night was the only place he could hear himself think. He surveyed his desk gloomily. Yesterday *should have* been the opening ceremony for the Chambers Program, and to-day the actual program would have officially commenced. He still couldn't digest it. The Chambers Program *always* had to start with the Foundation ceremony. It took place every year at exactly 1:00pm in the Arrangement Hall of the Foundation Vault and it *had* to be on the 17th of Tammuz. It wasn't a date that you could just change or take a 'rain check' on. The Urim Arch 'functioned' for precisely two hours and six minutes once a year and that was it. If you missed it, then you'd just have to sit back and wait another year. That's why Ezra had meticulously prepared for the Foundation ceremony even though this time he knew it was ludicrous and would never take place. This 17th of Tammuz was lost . . . .

He gazed at his piles and then divided up the stack of lion banners and insignia badges. He had taken into account that most of the Chamber One initiates would end up being from the tribe of Judah and he would have distributed most of these at yesterday's ceremony. It was also why the stack with the lion symbols was the tallest and now starting to slope. To make space, he started shifting the piles slightly and then picked up one of the small insignias of Dan. It was common knowledge that ten out of the twelve tribes were lost over 2,500 years ago after the northern Kingdom was conquered by the Assyrians. The popular consensus was that only two tribes survived—Judah and Levi. Little did people know that they had now found members from *six* out of the ten lost tribes; Simeon, Benjamin, Menashe, Asher, Zevulun and Dan. But, it was only by having students pass under the Urim Arch that they'd discover that all-important fact. Now that they missed the Foundation ceremony, how would Daniel ever know how to arrange the students? Except for the students' clearly visible gender, Ezra and Daniel were both blind as bats. West quadrant had the girls, East Quadrant had the boys, but positioning the kids *within* their own unique and respective groups was vital to the entire Chambers Program.

Ezra's piles were of course impeccably arranged; Levites in the center, Benjamin and Menashe to the west, Asher and Dan in the north, Simeon in the south, Judah and Zevulun to the east. He carefully put the insignia of Dan back where it belonged in the north and instantly turned nostalgic when he remembered Devorah Barak's ceremony nine years before.

It was one of their largest groups of Chamber One initiates and Devorah had shyly moved to the end of the line to make sure she was last. The studious young girl looked like she had never smiled a day in her life. Her eyes were always cast downward looking at the floor and not without good reason. Devorah's family had walked hundreds of miles after they escaped Ethiopia's capital city of Addis Ababa to reach the Sudanese border where a clandestine rescue team awaited them from the 'Land of King Solomon and Queen Sheba'. The trek had been too treacherous, too dangerous and too long, and Devorah's pregnant mother and a younger brother had died on the way. But, when Devorah passed under the Urim Arch, the fiery letters burst forth in a color that they had never seen before and two emblazoned Hebrew letters were as clear as day for everyone to read. There she was—their first confirmed descendant from the lost tribe of Dan.

The kids from all seven chambers broke ranks wildly. The girls rushed toward Devorah encircling her in a mob-like hug, and then they picked her up and carried

her on high. Everyone was cheering loudly and excitedly. Ezra had never seen a brighter or happier smile on a
student's face in his entire career, and the best part was
that smile was still there. He remembered how his own
hands couldn't stop shaking when he gave Devorah the
deep blue banner of Dan with its snake insignia. They
had found five more descendants of the tribe of Dan since
then. But, as he re-focused on his desk, it was sorely obvious that there were still too many single banners and
badges that hadn't been claimed.

On the other hand, Ezra could only *wish* that they'd
find *another* initiate on whom to bestow the black banner
with the unicorn-looking oryx. His hands were more
than full with Jason Reid who was more outside of his
classroom than inside it due to his 'distinctive' sense of
humor. His parents were originally from Salt Lake City,
and their ancestors were conclusively from here, because
when Jason roller-skated under the Urim Arch, another
one of the ten lost tribes had been found. Ezra *always*
checked the bottom of sneakers after that fiasco. But,
there was no doubt about it, a long lost descendant of Joseph—more specifically, the tribe of Menashe had joined
the ranks, and he was still the *only* one. Ezra knew that
the school's faculty, Jason's parents and probably Jason
himself were stupefied as to why he was never expelled.

And then there were of course those painfully dis-
appointing moments with the Kohens and Levis: kids
who had been brought up their whole lives thinking they
were the priestly elite, only to find out they were from
the tribe of Judah. Ezra had allocated five Levi banners
and insignias for this year's Foundation ceremony. He
picked up the beautiful banner from the center of his
desk. It was one third white, one third black, and one

third red with a picture of the Choshen, the oracle that included the names of every tribe and held the mysterious Urim V'Tumim. He sighed to himself. 'Enlightenment' also had its drawbacks, and Ezra knew what it was like when your own personal bubble of illusion was popped. It was 'Oholiov from the tribe of *Dan*' that was named as Bezalel's assistant over 3,000 years ago, but unlike his namesake, Ezra wore the lion of Judah insignia.

He would have loved to gather crowds of people from the Western Wall plaza, usher them into the Arrangement Hall, and then have them walk single file through the Urim Arch to see what might turn up. Maybe they'd finally find a member of one of the four tribes that were still lost, but without Daniel, he couldn't even access the Foundation Vault. He started to carefully pack away all the banners and insignias. It really didn't make a difference anymore. Now, they were all lost.

CHAPTER 7

Seas of Misery

Tamar Davidson crossed the last number off her list and then crumpled it into a ball. "Only soccer camp still has openings."

"Absolutely *not*! What happened to that science museum camp?"

"Full. We can register him today for two summers from now...," Tamar groaned as she threw the ball into the garbage. "You were supposed to take care of computer camp. *You* said 'no problem'."

"Well, that's *before* I knew that it started ten days ago. Is it my fault that they don't take late registration?" Jessie shook his head unhappily as he wrapped his sandwich neatly into a napkin. "Wait! I know! The Zoological Studies Seminar! What happened to that?"

"It's called *Zoo Camp* Jessie! And we're wait-listed."

With a crick of his neck, Jessie carefully put his lunch into his briefcase as Tamar reluctantly went back to the Friday cleaning detail. But it was more like re-sorting the mega-mess and her mood was plummeting quickly when Elisha came into the kitchen and asked her the *same* question for the umpteenth time. She started losing her patience.

"I *told* you Saturday night. How *many times* do I have to tell you that?"

Elisha moped as he walked away from his annoyed mother. *Well at least Aaron was coming back.* And there weren't any notes left around to make it seem like it was a permanent disappearing act. But he'd only believe it when he saw it, because he had seen Aaron's face before he had walked straight out of his room and then *out* of the house.

Tamar's only focus was her collection of disheveled newspapers, grubby pacifiers trailing dust wisps, and a bottle slopping curdled goop she had pulled out from under the sofa. From the corner of her eye she could see that Elisha was staring listlessly at the door. She momentarily held back her rising aggravation. It wasn't like she hadn't sensed his loneliness.

"Finish vacuum cleaning and dusting the living room and then you can invite a friend over." She was surprised when Elisha didn't even want one.

Keren kept buzzing him through the phone intercom and now he was really annoyed, but he still answered in his calm, but firm psychologist's voice.

"I believe I made it quite clear there were to be *no* interruptions this morning."

Dr. Brody absolutely hated working on Fridays, but with a fully-booked patient schedule Sunday to Thursday, it was the only day he had left to handle the paperwork and catch up on the messy cases. He went back to his laptop and continued writing notes while listening to the recording of Jonathan's last hypnosis session. He needed to concentrate because he was in a major quandary after the police fiasco and still couldn't decide what to do. He was determined that today would be *it*. He would carefully analyze Jonathan's recording and would either establish or disqualify False Memory Syndrome. One way or another, once and for all, enough was enough. Dr. Brody hit play again and was immediately swept away by his work. Jonathan's new neurotic obsession to only focus on the Seventh Chamber might have been a major tactical error with the police, but he hadn't been this excited about a case in years. It was mind boggling really. It was as if he had entered into a separate reality, and even though it was pure fabrication, it was still highly entertaining. He skipped over what he still considered the incessantly *long* chanting of syllables and then listened some more.

> *In the Chamber of the Door of Pure Marble Stone, the Watcher is casting thousands upon thousands of waves of water. When the lightning strikes, I can see that the Merkavah is waiting to transport me. The four dimensional faces of the lion, ox and eagle are like exploding torches and the noise from their wings sounds like a tidal wave crashing.*

The phone intercom buzzed again.

Keren's voice was stressed. "Sorry Dr. Brody, but the Chief Surgeon of Mt. Scopus has called urgently three times and he's on hold waiting to speak to you."

Dr. Brody reluctantly took the call. When he got off, he pushed aside all the work on his desk. He quickly checked his calendar and date book and then went over to his panoramic window which gave an expansive bird's eye view of Tel Aviv's city park. He stared at the busy activity below and tried to gather his thoughts. How had he allowed himself to be *so* blinded by this case? *How?*

He stared at the phone. It wasn't the first time he had given a phone consultation to Chief Surgeon Goldman at Mount Scopus, but this one caught him entirely off guard. He had first suggested that they use sodium amobarbital on the patient, but they had already tried it without success. So, the answer was 'no', hypnosis was rarely successful with amnesia resulting from a head injury. And, 'no', he couldn't help Chief Goldman with his *personal VIP patient*, and sorry, 'no', not even if he was a close friend of the family . . . and NO, not even if he was a brilliant physics professor at Cambridge knighted *Sir* by the Queen of England herself.

Dr. Brody checked the dates again. They still matched *exactly*. Jonathan, of course, had never bothered to mention that he had 'curiously' developed his own amnesia right at the exact *same time* as Professor Bezalel! Goodbye Chief Goldman and goodbye case of a lifetime!

Now it was all too clear in Dr. Brody's mind. He rose from his desk and headed back to gaze out of his windows. He was looking at a simple case of introjection. A glaringly obvious one—Jonathan's subconscious mind had identified *so strongly* with his mentor and teacher's amnesia that he had actually developed his *own* amnesia. The rest was just the usual standard defense mechanisms of a fertile mind, and Jonathan had created an entire fantasy world in order to cope with the pain and loss. Dr. Brody winced. The diagnosis was as basic as one of those deplorable 'Psychology for Dummies' books.

He would confront Jonathan with the information at their next meeting, but there was no doubt that he would regrettably have to refer him to a good therapist. He remembered the tall detective laughing out loud, 'What a joke', and cringed with self-disgust.

But then Dr. Brody's thoughts shifted to Professor Bezalel. He imagined that he must be a highly charismatic personality if he was able to have such a strong effect on Jonathan Marks who was brilliant in his own right. And, well, even Chief Surgeon Goldman regarded him as a *personal* VIP patient. Dr. Brody had done his homework on Sir-Professor Bezalel the previous Friday. The man was Google-glutted and had quite a wide Wiki spread. He had attained something of a physics guru status at Cambridge due to some revolutionary new physics theory. But, unfortunately, despite many searches, Dr. Brody was unable to find any details of Professor Bezalel's theory work online. He ended up having to call in a professional favor from a colleague on Sabbatical at Cambridge. Nothing had arrived yet, but certainly everything about this enigmatic man seemed impressive and beyond reproach, and Dr. Brody could only sigh at his present condition, which was highly unfortunate but most probably temporary. The only strange business was *why* in the world someone who had his qualifications would want to be an elementary and high school teacher?? In Dr. Brody's opinion, that was a horrendous vocation and a grotesque waste of time for someone with that talent. And then there was the proof of where it got you, instead of that romantically noble pursuit of molding impressionable young minds, you ended up with a psychopathic teacher's pet that went over the edge.

The Davidsons were in the midst of eating their traditional Saturday night pizza when Aaron showed up with a small duffle bag and joined in very naturally. It was almost like he was already part of the family. But Elisha's father barely let everyone take two enjoyable bites before he made sure to bring up the computer lessons again and then went into a long-winded explanation of how, "Without computer literacy today you might as well be illiterate on the job market." He had it all mapped out. Aaron would move boxes for three weeks while Elisha tutored him and then he'd move him into their computerized archive data entry division. From there, the sky was the limit. He could even transcribe manuscripts.

Elisha just couldn't see it. And it really surprised him when Aaron was actually raring to go for his first lesson right after the pizza.

A very self-satisfied Jessie looked at Tamar and said loudly, "You see, computer camp orientation has already begun."

Tamar was forcing the cardboard pizza box into the garbage and mumbled, "It's still not a solution."

Aaron dragged a kitchen chair into Elisha's room and set it down next to his small desk. Elisha was really hoping that it was a ploy and that Aaron had changed his mind and now he'd be just as eager as he was to experiment more with the mirror stone, but his first words were, "I hope you haven't been messin' around with that thing again, have you?"

Elisha shook his head no. "You told me not to do it myself, so I've been waiting for you, like you said."

"For *me*?" Aaron grimaced. "Hey. Whooooah—I didn't tell you to wait for *me* . . . , I just told you, you shouldn't be doin' it yourself."

Elisha continued innocently, "So that's why I've been waiting for you. 'Cause you see I have a plan, 'cause I was thinking, well I know someone who I think can help us. Rav Kadosh. He's a Mekubal. You know him?"

Aaron didn't like the 'us' word, but he still snorted out a loud laugh. In the entire time he had been 'working' the Wall, he hadn't seen that mysterious Rav come out even *once*. And that was what, say on and off for about four years now . . . He was happy to throw a wrench into the whole subject. "Sure, and why don't you ask the President of the United States too while you're at it. That man is just as unreachable, trust me." He rubbed his hands together and said, "Come on, teach me."

Elisha stared at him in disbelief. Had he really fallen that fast under his parents' influence?

Aaron looked him right in the eye and said, "Hey listen up, you heard your parents. This is 'computer camp', not Camp Twilight Zone, okay!"

He *had*, and Elisha begrudgingly began with the real basics, but Aaron looked like he would be more comfortable picking up his desk rather than sitting cramped and uncomfortable alongside it. His hands and fingers were so big too, that Elisha couldn't ever see him using the keyboard well. But, he carried on with the job even though Aaron was really impatient.

"Geez, get serious, don't you have any games or somethin' you can teach me? How is it you kids spend so many hours on computers if you're not doin' somethin' fun?"

Elisha smiled, but, he couldn't see starting Aaron on Flightpilot just yet.

"Well, what kind of games do you like?" Elisha asked.

"Card games. Don't you have any card games?"

Elisha thought hard and then remembered there

was an old-fashioned game that all the school's secretaries used to play on their breaks called 'FreeCell'. Aaron caught on very quickly and then wouldn't relinquish the keyboard. Elisha kept trying to shift his focus back onto the mirror stone, but it was as if he had lost all interest. He couldn't understand Aaron at all and ended up asking in total frustration, "Don't you *want* to know what all of this is about?"

Aaron completely ignored him and said he was on a 'winnin' streak'. It wasn't that he hadn't heard the question, but how do you break it to such a young kid that sometimes you're just *much* better off *not* knowing. Aaron had gotten his lucky sign last week, and as far as the rest was concerned . . . *just let sleeping dogs lie.*

Aaron's winning streak went on for over an hour while Elisha became increasingly bored and antsy.

"What about Rav Kadosh, are we going to go there tomorrow, or not?"

"Yeah, yeah, after I finish playin', we'll go"

"No. I mean tomorrow?"

"Yeah, yeah, we'll go tomorrow," Aaron said.

But Elisha was fairly sure that he hadn't even heard the question and it took a whole hour more before Aaron finally gave him his room back.

Elisha felt totally aggravated as he changed into one of his old ripped up sleeping T-shirts until he noticed that he could definitely feel the hot summer air coming through his window. That was weird. The mirror stone didn't seem to be blowing out cold air anymore. He went over to double check. The stone even felt warm. It was the first night since he had shared his room with the thing that he didn't need to cover it. He wondered if it had to do with Aaron spending so much time in his room? Maybe it was worth giving the Priest of Light FreeCell lessons.

It was so very peaceful and silent in the Davidson household that night that even the mirror stone changed its surface without the slightest sound. The rock hard surface lost all of its solidity, and in its place hung a wall of red flowing blood. It would have seemed like a fluid red river just suspended on the wall, except that every so often something extremely large and black and smooth would bulge out half way across the room as it tried to sliver free from the crimson glistening waters.

In the thick blackness, two massive eyelids slowly opened. They revealed two forceful dark grey tornadoes that were whirling ominously. In the complete silence the blackness swelled as it deeply breathed in the air of the Eighth Kingdom. It could instantly smell that its prey was sleeping. Even though 2,846 years had gone by since it had seen a human, it still remembered how easy it was to kill one.

Aaron woke up startled. He ran toward Elisha's room, but he wasn't quick enough. Elisha's screams were piercing through the darkened hallways. The Davidsons had toppled out of their bedroom with anxious faces and met Aaron charging into the hallway at the same time. Elisha smashed into everyone with good speed and grabbed both of his parents at their waists.

Jessie was completely flustered at the embarrassing display of their family problems. He apologized to Aaron in an irritable and hoarse voice that hadn't woken up yet. "Sorry. He's got these . . . sleeping disturbances."

"Oh, nightmares," Aaron said sounding relieved, "I thought we were under attack," and he chuckled light-heartedly. He hesitated a moment, headed back to the guest room, and then changed directions and walked into the kitchen instead to make himself a cup of strong black coffee.

"Elisha, are you alright?" asked his mother with intense concern in her voice.

Elisha nodded, and was doing his best to hide his sweating and shaking.

"You nearly scared us half to death, *again*," said his father as he started pushing him back toward his room, but Elisha dug his heels into the floor.

"I'm *not* going back in there."

His parents exchanged exasperated looks. Elisha's mother pulled at her bathrobe while leading Elisha into the living room. She plopped down comfortably on the sofa and asked with a yawn, "Was it another nightmare?"

Elisha's sleepy looking face seemed frozen when he answered, "I don't know." But he probably should have said that it was just *a large deadly sleeping disturbance*.

Aaron came out of the kitchen with his fresh brewed coffee and looked at the Davidsons' tired, disoriented faces. They were practically falling asleep on the sofa. Actually, Jessie was already asleep while Elisha was sitting upright and rigid, sandwiched right between the two of them. Aaron eagerly offered to help.

"Hey listen, don't you folks worry, I'm a born insomniac. I can stay up with the boy for a bit."

Both of Elisha's parents were reluctant, but then again the thought of getting back into bed was *very* attractive. Jessie looked at his watch and was already off the sofa, "I do have an early start in the morning." Tamar had already resigned herself to another sleepless night until Elisha surprisingly nodded eagerly that it was okay and even seemed to *want* Aaron to keep him company. It was a done deal. In the dimly lit living room, she hadn't really seen the utter terror on Elisha's face.

Aaron sat himself down in the recliner chair and lined up a stack of cookies on the arm rest. He was dunking the last one into his coffee when Elisha finally spoke up. His voice was trembling.

"I do know. There was something . . . ." he hesitated but then went on, "something black and large and swimming in blood coming from the stone. I'm telling you something huge and black and it was in a pool of *blood*." His body shuddered and his teeth chattered, but he still managed to say what was really terrifying him. "I think it was coming *out. I know it was.*"

Aaron walked across the living room and pushed at Elisha's shoulder to force him to get up. He could feel Elisha's whole body shaking, but Aaron was determined. "Come on," he said and directed him back toward his bedroom. Aaron turned on the bright ceiling light, and cautiously went over to inspect the mirror-stone. It was the same old slab of stone as it ever was. Elisha was staring at it in horror from his bedroom doorway.

"Do you still see it?' Aaron asked.

"*No*. Do you?" Elisha answered sarcastically. He wasn't about to be persuaded that it was all a dream or only in his head.

Aaron could tell that seeing the stone back in its usual form did absolutely nothing to allay Elisha's fear. He strengthened his grip on Elisha and almost hated himself for what he said next. "Well, it was just a nightmare Elisha, 'cause you see, look around—perfectly normal mirror stone—perfectly normal room. It didn't happen. End of nightmare story." He rapped hard on the mirror-stone surface. "You see? It's solid as a rock."

"Really??!! *Sure.* Perfectly normal stone! You don't believe that for a second, why are you even talking like *that*?" Elisha pulled away from Aaron with force.

Aaron didn't know who he was fooling. He sat down exhausted and admitted, "Okay. So, you're right. And you know what—?"

"Cover it!" Elisha practically shouted out. "I usually cover it with that blanket over there." Elisha pointed to it from the doorway.

Aaron draped the thick blanket over the stone thinking it couldn't hurt to humor the kid, but he still mumbled to himself, "Like this is gonna really do somethin' . . . ." He then turned to Elisha and asked, "When were you gonna go see that Rav Kadosh?"

"We can go tomorrow morning, early."

Aaron stared at the floor gripped with a primal fear. Being silent was cruel and he knew it. But for some reason, Aaron just didn't want to tell him that he had dreamed the same thing that Elisha had seen, which was why he had woken up and had run to his room. Maybe his insanity was contagious, or maybe admitting he had seen it would make him insane. No, he *knew* what it was. The kid was waking up ALL the sleeping dogs and now he'd need to '*Let go*' again. He shook off his own irritation for the kid's sake and tried the good old lift-the-spirit voice.

"Come on Elisha, why don't you camp out in the livin' room for the night."

But Elisha's caustic mood couldn't be broken. "Why? Everything's just fine in here. It's not like I can die a horrible death from my own imagination, right?"

Aaron got to his feet and headed out the door. He didn't need to look behind him to see that if Elisha was any closer to him he'd be standing on his heels.

Jonathan's head was throbbing, but he couldn't be more elated. He had maintained his non-verbal consciousness for five hours and at one point he even thought of stretching it to a full eight, except that he knew it would take him another three hours to return—the usual infinity hangover, and he still had to maintain some minimal work functionability. He microwaved two pieces of day-old pizza and went to fill the bath. Every one of his limbs ached and he could still hear the low buzzing sound of *Ophanim* like a distant memory. The bathtub was halfway full when he spotted a small cockroach floating in the middle. He mused. Should he? He couldn't help himself, so he tried. He focused all his innate concentration on the difficult permutation incantation, but instead, the rushing water from the bathtub faucet immediately stopped flowing. He lowered his head carefully, rubbed his temples and concentrated again on the permutations. Now there was a tiny goldfish convulsing on his bathroom floor. With a frustrated glare he returned it to its Source. His clumsiness only made him more determined. He focused on the bathtub with every molecule in his mind and then exhaled with ecstatic force. He knew it was childish—but this time it worked. The cockroach was now laying stomach up on dry surface in the middle of Jonathan Mark's porcelain white bathtub. There were two walls of crystal clear water congealed like glass panes on each side of it. Jonathan smiled and took some toilet paper and disposed of the corpse. He spent most of the night trying to reunite the small body of water, but as many times as he refilled his bathtub, there was always that sliver of a section that remained water-free. He gave up at 4:00am and took a shower, even thought there was a distinctive split in the stream of hot water spraying down from the showerhead.

Mr. Davidson's 5:00am chorus of alarm clocks didn't wake Elisha up. He was already dressed and in the guest room trying to wake Aaron up.

"Aaron get up. Come on. *Get* up! We've got to go and see Rav Kadosh."

Aaron was exhausted and mumbled, "What are you *crazy*, at this hour?"

Elisha could barely budge the mammoth sleepy body, and couldn't understand how adults could be such immovable logs. Elisha could tell that Aaron was intentionally resisting. Had the Kohen of Light suddenly changed his mind?

Actually, in the sanity of waking consciousness, Aaron did have a change of heart. He was sure that if they even miraculously got an audience with the legendary Rav, he would just laugh in both of their faces, and he'd had enough of that in his own lifetime. He rolled over with a definite snore and it was only after Elisha resorted to non-stop harassment that Aaron finally got out of bed, but he flatly refused to go in and see the Rav. With all seriousness, Aaron warned, "Okay. Let's get this straight. I'm goin' with you, but I'm *not* goin' into the Rav with you. You've got that? So, don't go *kvetchin'* again once we're down there."

Mr. Davidson was totally surprised that he would be joined by his young son *and* his new house guest for 'sunrise'. They were just sitting there on the sofa dressed, ready and waiting for him. With a fleeting guilty thought, he hoped that Aaron hadn't stayed up all night with Elisha. He unfortunately knew he'd have to inquire about some professional help for his son. Tamar had convinced him. But Jessie had zero respect for the behavioral sciences, and it wasn't because he was, in Tamar's words, 'full of inhibitions and backwards'. It was quite the opposite. It was because he knew that the field of psychology wasn't even *remotely* scientific. When it came to the mind, even the best of them were all just fumbling in the dark. He looked at the sofa again and felt satisfied. 'Early to rise' was always his motto and certainly what he was seeing in front of him was an outstanding display of positive behavior! And it was always nice to share the beauty of the quiet Jerusalem stone streets at this special hour especially if those accompanying you were too tired to speak.

When they reached the Kotel Plaza, Mr. Davidson silently rushed off to his spot near the Wall just as Elisha started to worry. He still wasn't entirely sure how he had gotten to Rav Kadosh the first time around and he just had the strongest feeling that this time wasn't going to be any easier. He was wrong.

This time the ancient stairway was well lit, and he could see a wide ramp-way running alongside it, and there were even *people. This is nice and normal*, Elisha thought even though there was no sign of an elevator. He kindly asked them if they could direct him to Rav Kadosh's room. A tall man looked down suspiciously at Elisha.

"It's right through that door on the left."

Easy enough, thought Elisha. He pushed open a double solid wood door and was completely disoriented. He had entered a massive waiting area with lots of mismatched chairs lined up against the walls. Most of the seats were taken, and many people were standing. The room was full of men, women and children of all ages. *What were they all doing here at such a strange hour of the morning?* There was a man sitting at a desk at the far end who clearly seemed to be playing the role of receptionist. Elisha went over to him and politely asked,

"Excuse me sir, could you please tell me where I can find Rav Kadosh?"

The man's answer was acerbic and abrupt as he rolled his eyes and said, "Here!" at the ridiculously obvious.

Elisha realized he was supposed to feel incredibly stupid, but he had no choice but to subject himself to more. "So, can I see him?"

The man had on a worn expression of having vast experience of dealing with lots of stupid people. He sighed as if he had been asked to perform a strenuous task, and tapped his finger loudly on what Elisha had to admit was a very large sign on the front of his desk in bold letters.

Elisha quietly read to himself.

Rav Kadosh receives the public on Sunday mornings from 4:00am to 9:00am

The man was already waiting impatiently with a pen in hand as if it had taken Elisha an exorbitantly long amount of time to read the sign. "Write your name on that list on the wall. First come first served."

Elisha saw three sheets of plain white paper taped to the wall. It was a list of people's names with a number on the side. The first and second pages were already full. The third page was half way full. Elisha went to add his name to the bottom of the list. He was number 42! *How long would that take!!* He looked back at the first page, there were only two names crossed off. He resigned himself to a wait, and a long one at that. It occurred to him that getting to the Rav last time might not have been easier, but it had definitely been much *quicker*.

With sheer boredom instantly descending upon him, Elisha started studying the other people in the room. There was a married couple looking very worried and holding each other's hands. Next to them was a boy that looked to be his age. He was sitting in a wheelchair and his whole body was deformed, Elisha quickly shifted his attention. There were three men to the right who were all bent over an open Talmud and right behind them was a woman knitting away. Elisha opened his pouch, even though he knew he had nothing in it to bide his time. He wished he had brought a game and then thought he might just doze off in his seat.

He stared at the ceiling and then into the far corner of the room thinking he should just go. He recognized the face in the corner, it was Sarah Weizman, or 'Sicko Sarah' as the mean kids in the neighborhood would call her. She was about two years older than Elisha. Her mouth was always mumbling and she was constantly pulling at her own hair, and the reason she got the name wasn't only because she was sick, but because she was really *weird* looking. But Elisha knew way better than to call *her* any names. In his house that would be breaking one of the 'Ten Commandments' and punishable by the most disapproving face his mother owned, that and never being able to choose his own breakfast cereal again. Sarah was severely autistic, and Elisha's mother was a special education teacher whose life was dedicated to autistic children. Elisha watched as an old man with a long white beard was being wheeled in right next to her. He thought sadly of Saba Gabriel. He wouldn't even have to be here now

if he was still alive. The wheelchair blocked his view of
Sarah. That was better. Then he remembered how Saba
Gabriel used to stand up out of respect whenever he saw
an autistic kid. He said they were special, and so did his
mother. Elisha couldn't see it and he shifted his attention
to Sarah's mother because *she* looked like a real-life fairy
tale princess off the pages of one of his storybooks. It
was so strange that Sarah could even be her daughter. He
knew it was rude to stare, but since her eyes were closed,
he continued to. There were tears running down her face.

The loud sound of a bag dropping to the floor shifted his and everyone else's attention to a young mother
clumsily entering the room. She was holding a baby about
Shira's age and couldn't seem to control anything she was
carrying. As she bent down to pick up her bag, a bottle
rolled across the floor, and by the time she retrieved that,
her keys and sunglasses had fallen out the other side.
There were at least three people who had come to her
aid to restore order. Other than that, she seemed to know
exactly what she was doing as she went straight for the
list on the wall to add her name. She must be a regular,
Elisha thought. As she came closer, Elisha could tell that
the little girl looked a lot like Shira, until a terrible difference became shockingly obvious. This little girl had
no arms. She had nothing where her arms were supposed
to be! Like a factory oversight at a doll shop. Elisha felt
a deep stab in his chest. She was going to be number
43! And how was that ever going to help her? And then
Elisha finally did 'get it'. He wasn't the *only* one with a
problem. This whole room was *filled* with them! His own
horror-movie nightmare suddenly seemed stupid in this
sea of misery room.

He angrily clutched Rav Kadosh's calling card and

got up to leave when an elderly hand softly patted his shoulder. With a quick glance up, he saw that it belonged to a curious looking old woman who all at once seemed radiantly kind and yet someone you didn't even *think* of messing with. She sweetly and firmly said in a loud voice,

"The Rav will see you now."

What? But, how could that be? Elisha thought. He didn't know what to say, and he heard himself dumbly stammering, "Uh, but, I, uh . . . I'm number 42."

The people in the room were clearly upset as well, but this elderly matron seemed to have experience in lynch control as she waved her hands and started speaking in several different languages to him and the onlookers.

"Silly boy, as if the Rav's grandson has to take a number!" She winked in Elisha's direction.

It was actually a good line, he had to admit, because everyone around the room started smiling instead, except the man behind the desk who looked like he had swallowed a frog, but if he knew any better he certainly wasn't going to say a thing.

Elisha was escorted into the Rav's study. It was exactly how he had remembered it from the last time, just a different entrance. He felt so relieved to see Rav Kadosh, but then felt quickly obliged to mind his manners and blurted out, "I don't mind waiting."

The Rav was quick to respond, "But, I do. Do you have the Shamir?"

Elisha hesitated for a split second. Why did he keep asking him that? Was the slimy, bloody, black disgusting horror thing the Shamir? *It couldn't be.* But he knew from last time that he would have to speak fast, and without being able to control it, he also found himself shaking when he did. "No. Some kind of snake monster came out of the mirror stone last night. It was in a pool of blood and I have this . . . ."

"*What mirror stone?*" Rav Kadosh impatiently interrupted him. He then set an accusatory eye on Elisha and demanded, "*Elisha Davidson*, why is it that you *never* mentioned a mirror stone before?"

Rav Kadosh's face suddenly seemed to be afire with understanding but also extremely upset. Nervousness was getting the best of Elisha, and he started rambling quickly.

"The mirror stone in my room, that's how I got the Choshen stone."

Even Elisha was amazed at himself that he had left out this all important detail the last time around, but really, Rav Kadosh had never given him the chance to catch his breath. And it was obvious that this time he had to be quick too, so he wasn't going to mess up on the details again. "And the Kohen of Light gave me this," Elisha said speedily as he swiftly pulled out the triangle.

Rav Kadosh looked shocked, but then took the object in his hands right away and closed his eyes. He had an expression that showed he knew exactly what it was. Elisha's eyes widened waiting for the answer.

"Selflessness," he announced with satisfaction and then peeled off the tape and handed back to Elisha a perfectly fixed triangle.

Elisha was totally confused.

"Elisha, what time are your parents *NOT* at home today?"

Now Elisha was even more baffled. *That's the question he's asking?* But he automatically answered anyway.

The Rav quickly commanded, "Go home Elisha."

What? Did he hear right? Go home? Elisha couldn't move. He was being thrown out and there was that black blood thing. He couldn't leave now, he again hadn't explained things well, *the thing was coming out*. And why were the conversations in this place so frustrating?

"Elisha, I'll be there at 9:15. But the Kohen absolutely *must* be there with you!"

Elisha was nodding frantically as his whole body lightened up and practically shot to the sky. But there it was again, the horrible image of the Rav looking like he had doubled in age. It was terrifying and instantly made him very eager to leave. Elisha said more than one thank you as he walked as fast as he could out of the room, but by the time he got to the stairs he was running and practically collided directly into Aaron at the lower entrance. Aaron seemed quite surprised to see him.

"Well, that didn't take very long. I heard someone sayin' that there was a three week wait up there."

"There was!" said Elisha with a cryptic smirk that turned into an I-won-the-lottery smile.

It always amazed Aaron to see just how resilient kids could be. A few hours ago, it wasn't unreasonable to think that the kid might need lots of expensive therapy to get over the bloodbath trauma, and here he was suddenly walking on sunshine without the slightest wear and tear for it. It definitely caught all of Aaron's curiosity, but he played it cool.

"Well, didn't your mother teach you to wait your turn? What? Did you just bulldozer right . . . ." Suddenly Aaron was interrupted.

"*Heyyyy, Madman,* whacha up to?"

Elisha saw an old, smiling, wrinkly-faced man that had horribly disheveled grey hair wrapped around his head like wisps of cotton candy. The man took hold of Aaron's hands and gave him a big smile, and as far as

Elisha could tell, there weren't too many teeth left in his mouth.

"Hey Eliyahu, you're still alive. Where have you been all this time?" Aaron asked good-naturedly.

"Oh, me usual, cleaning up afder all da messy, gabbage dumpin' dourists on da plaza and in da dunnels."

Elisha could tell that Aaron couldn't seem to shake off his old friend's grip as the man started groping in a large burlap bag he was holding and quickly pulled out a handful of small pieces of paper. Elisha noticed that his hand was even blacker than Aaron's had been the first night he saw him.

"Com'on Madman, pick one," the man said as he shook the bag and moved it closer and closer to Aaron's face. "You *gotta* pick one."

It was clear to Elisha that the rolled and scrunched up pieces of paper were from the Western Wall. There were hundreds or maybe even thousands of these tiny prayer notes being placed, pressed and forced between the cracks of the ancient stones day after day by Israelis and tourists from all over the world. Even kings, queens and US presidents had put notes in the wall. That's how the Wall also got its other name—The *Wailing* Wall. Elisha felt sure that he was watching some kind of weird beggar ritual as Aaron chose one of the tiny folded pieces of paper. Now Eliyahu was waving his hand in Elisha's face.

"You're Madman's friend, so you can pick one too."

Elisha did, but was careful not to touch any part of Eliyahu's hand.

"I hope yah got a good one," Eliyahu said as he waited and grinned expectantly.

Aaron still seemed in a rush to shake him off. "Well, it was nice seein' yah around. Keep up the good work for all of us!" he said as he patted Eliyahu on the back.

Eliyahu seemed extremely disappointed. "Watcha not gonna read it now?"

With a, "later", Aaron turned in the opposite direction and pulled Elisha to walk away. Elisha practically had to run to keep up with Aaron's fast pace and honestly couldn't believe his ears. Were they actually going to randomly pick notes from the Wall and *read* them? They belonged in the Wall. And it would be like reading some else's private personal mail. Is that what the beggars spent their time doing? Elisha was definitely going to return his note unopened to one of the Wall cracks at his next visit. Running alongside Aaron, Elisha held up his note and asked, "What do you do with these?" But Elisha could see that Aaron had already finished reading his and was pocketing it.

"Forget about that. Well? Did you see him or not?"

Elisha's excitement came back full force. "You're not going to believe it, but he's going to come to *us*! He's coming to the house to see the stone for himself!"

Aaron seemed unsure he heard right.

"Come on, isn't that like the best?!" Elisha smiled.

It actually was, and Aaron stopped for a moment wondering if just maybe there was one respectable normal person in the world he could tell his visions to who wouldn't laugh in his face. Maybe this Rav was the one. Despite himself, Aaron was starting to feel hopeful. Even though by now, he had certainly learned never to hope for too much of anything, especially if he ever got the slightest hope that there might be hope, because that's when he could be sure that it was hopeless.

CHAPTER 8

Ispaklaria

By the time they got home, Shira was already making lots of annoying fussing sounds in her crib and it was only 6:30am. *Mom's probably still sleeping. Let her sleep*, Elisha thought. He picked up cuddly Shira in her footsy pajamas. She was so excited to be released from her crib prison that her feet were kicking wildly. Elisha hugged her arms tightly and clapped her hands. And yup she had them, squishy fatso baby hands that he had never thought twice about until then. But he was too late to avoid her sopping wet diaper which had already ruined his T-shirt. That was the thing about babies. Yeah, they were cute, but they did so many gross things that parents would never admit were gross. His first instinct was to get mad and put her right back in the crib, but for a split second he got why parents were like that, and he even surprised himself when he sounded almost like his mother when he said, "Okay, let's get you a bottle and a clean diaper." But, it was easier said than done. Shira was resisting his every move with those healthy hands.

In the background, Elisha could hear faint sounds of Aaron in the kitchen, opening the fridge and going through cabinets. His stomach startled to growl. He was famished. His mission accomplished with Shira, he found his way into the kitchen and was surprised to see that Aaron was already cooking up some pancakes. That was interesting. Aaron Kohen could cook. It seemed so regular considering that he was the Priest of Light.

Aaron noticed his expression and said, "Stare away if you want, but you're lookin' at the best field cook the army ever had. And I also do shapes." With that Aaron flipped a strange brown blob into a plate. "See. That's a fighter plane. My specialty."

Elisha couldn't see it for the life of him, maybe it was a UFO . . . and having heard a lot about Israeli army food, he also wasn't going to count on anything edible.

At 7:45am, Tamar Davidson woke up distressed that she had overslept. But the real shock came when she entered the kitchen to find a stack of pancakes and a clean and changed Shira. Her wide eyes and smile said it all.

"Now I could get used to this!" she said as she sat down and savored her first bite of the pancake. "Delicious! How did you get them so light and fluffy with no milk in the house?"

Aaron quickly made a gesture that his lips were sealed. "Military secret—us field cooks pride ourselves on being resourceful."

But Elisha caught sight of Shira's open milk formula which he *knew* he had closed. His stomach convulsed, because until then his Mom was right. But their mood must have been too good, because it awakened Elisha's mother sixth sense again. It's almost like she knew they were waiting for her to leave to work and she came back three times forgetting 'something' and eyeing them suspiciously. But the third time was the absolute last, and both Aaron and Elisha couldn't have been more relieved.

Elisha noticed that Aaron was waiting just as impatiently as he was for the arrival of the great Kabbalah Master. He kept nervously drumming his fingertips on the milk formula and to make it more annoying his feet were tapping to a different beat.

The windowless room was roughly circular. The ceiling was low. Its stones were darker black than any dungeon's. It was the perfect place to let in all the different types of light, no matter if it was day or night or light or dark, or if the sky was blue or grey or white or orange with purple. Only without any light could you see the reflections of the pure fiery light, but to see the reflections you first had to spread your own light on every side using your nothingness. Then the glowing light would shine from the middle with the special good light on top of it. Then you would turn to the right and find the brilliant light of shining glass, and above it the radiant black light that ate all the other light that you could only see near the shining light. The black light could blind your eyes forever if you didn't know how to see it. That was its way of warning you that you were too blind already.

The letters of fire had their own light. Sometimes they spoke. Sometimes they were quiet. Sometimes they destroyed all the sound around them. Sometimes they spoke so loud and fast that they would crack the sky and you would never see them. Sometimes they had color inside. They always had fire on the outside. The outside space was a higher light because that was where thought was. Sometimes only their colors would speak. Sometimes they were completely still like statues and you had to speak their light and it would be so bright that your eyes would close and you would still see them, but if you could look inside them, you could find the scintillating light where you could know the color of all the lights. But, even the stunning light was still very very very far away from the Infinite Light.

Rav Kadosh arrived at *exactly* 9:15. He walked straight over to Aaron while Elisha had to suppress a laugh. Rav Kadosh seemed half Aaron's height, but then he curiously bowed his head low to Aaron and said, "It's a privilege."

Aaron looked like he could have died of embarrassment, but Rav Kadosh continued to stare up at Aaron and then quite firmly said, "Stop fighting yourself and *let go!*"

Aaron seemed stunned, but also seemed to understand something that Elisha didn't.

Elisha quickly led the way to his room, which also happened to be a mess. He was so glad his parents weren't around for this. The Rav at least didn't seem to notice. He had gone directly to the mirror and seemed completely awestruck yet all aglow as he stood in front of the majestic stone piece.

"*Massive! Where* did you unearth this ancient treasure?"

Elisha cringed slightly and then answered, "Uh, the bathroom . . . we're renovating."

Rav Kadosh winced and then called out to Aaron and Elisha to join him. Elisha quickly noticed something really weird. The Rav and Aaron didn't have *any* reflection. How was that possible? And how come he hadn't noticed that about Aaron before? Did Aaron see it too? It was like Elisha was the only one standing in front of the mirror stone. Then the Rav put his hands on the stone and started a slow incantation using Hebrew letters. Elisha didn't dare interrupt and listened carefully to Rav Kadosh's chant. It was made up of syllables rather than words and Elisha had never heard anything like it before.

It was a gradual and blurry transition, but it definitely was happening before their very eyes. The mirror transformed itself into a pure aquamarine gem. Elisha had never seen a color blue like that. He had never ever seen anything so clear and perfect and by the looks of Aaron, he hadn't either. It was like a piece of heaven was suspended on his wall in all its brilliance. Aaron whistled while Elisha's mouth was left hanging open.

"Now *that*," said the Rav, pointing at the mirror stone, "is really what you have on the wall." He bounced triumphantly on his heels. "That is its true form!"

He must have thought that Elisha and Aaron understood what he was talking about, but they were just exchanging confused looks.

Rav Kadosh left them no time to wonder.

"This isn't a mirror and this isn't a stone. It is an *Ispaklaria*!"

Aaron and Elisha glanced blankly and meekly at each other.

Rav Kadosh seemed irritated. "An *Ispaklaria*! You mean to tell me that neither one of you know what an Ispaklaria is?"

Their faces showed that they obviously didn't.

Rav Kadosh seemed at a loss. "It's a . . . a clear lens of vision . . . a transcendental reflection."

That moved their expressions from blank to a dull stupidity.

Rav Kadosh just shook his head in disbelief and then pointed at the stone. "From now on, you will *forget* what you *thought* you knew about this world of ours," he said cryptically and then he lowered his voice to a loud whisper. "An Ispaklaria is like a tear in the veil, a crack in the wall . . . the world without its mask. The world with *no* illusions. An Ispaklaria is a reality *not* bound by the 'laws of nature'—NONE whatsoever—no dimensions of space, time or even being! That's what you have on your wall . . . and, for you Elisha, your 'mirror stone' will be more than just a reflection of the true reality, it can *be* ultimate reality."

Elisha's eyes were widening even though he had *no* idea what the Rav meant.

Rav Kadosh started waving his hands animatedly, "You must learn to think of the whole world as being just one BIG BLIND SPOT, except, *except* for here, on your wall. Now is that clear?"

It wasn't and Elisha just stood speechless and clueless, while Aaron looked totally frozen in his own confusion. Elisha was about to try and ask a question, but it was too late. Rav Kadosh had started another one of his one way conversations and no one dared interrupt.

"Now, I'm about to reveal things to you," he looked at both their faces and added, "that neither one of you can even understand." His eyes searched above, and he continued, "I am just a vessel of knowledge and the Infinite One chooses his receptacles."

Elisha was sure that he heard a sorry sigh in that last comment.

"Elisha and Aaron come to my side and look into

the Ispaklaria."

Elisha couldn't help looking at his own reflection. It was the only one there. It made him feel special.

Rav Kadosh noticed and quickly added, "Very bad! And worse than I thought. Where's the key?"

Elisha shrugged as Rav Kadosh pointed with a sigh to the metal triangle.

"The *key* to ultimate reality is in your very hands!"

Elisha had no idea what to do with himself. The Rav was calling his mirror stone an '*Ispaklaria*' and the triangle a *key*! Didn't he say that it was selflessness? He was *sure* that's what he had called it earlier this morning and he couldn't see anything that looked like a triangle-shaped keyhole anywhere in the stone. Feeling like a total idiot, Elisha awkwardly tried to make up for it by trying to put his hand through the stone like he had done the other day. But the silver triangle just smashed into the 'Ispaklaria' with a crashing sound. Rav Kadosh's face suddenly seemed aghast.

"*NOT* like that. Stop! Where's the Choshen stone?!!" Rav Kadosh pointed to the silver piece. "What do you think this gaping rectangular spot in the middle is for?"

Aaron rushed out of the room while Rav Kadosh stared without blinking at the triangle. He didn't have enough time to study the masterpiece when Elisha had come to him this morning, and unfortunately, he wouldn't have enough time now. But, it was haunting him relentlessly. There was something more than selflessness . . . more than a key . . . Could it possibly be that he had merited laying his eyes on the Urim V'Tumim?? There was only one human being who knew what they or it looked like or what they or it were and he was also the same one who had placed them in the original Choshen for his brother Aaron thousands of years ago. He immediately shook off his unsettling thoughts, assuring himself that it was impossible, just as Aaron whisked back into the room and dropped the Choshen stone like a hot potato into Elisha's hand. The two then exchanged meaningful looks like, 'why didn't you figure that one out?'

Once the rectangular stone rested perfectly in the middle of the triangle, tiny balls started forming on the edges and then a stream of fiery letters burst out in a blinding light from each of the openings. Elisha sneaked a glance at Aaron to see if he was going to run out of the room, but he seemed paralyzed instead. Elisha squinted his eyes tightly so he could watch for any new messages, but these letters weren't at all like the ones he had seen on the 17th of Tammuz. They were so bright they looked like they were made out of lightning, but they were also a lot smaller, they didn't have sound and they weren't in any language that Elisha recognized. They seemed more like symbols—strings of fiery rainbow-colored symbols and each string started radiating out until it settled in a distinct cone-shaped field of vision. Elisha counted them quickly. There were definitely twelve. One side of the triangle had three, one had four and another side had five. Twelve different streams of fiery symbols blazing out in every direction across his room. The number twelve quickly made him think about the twelve tribes on the Choshen. Maybe there was some kind of connection.

"Wrong connection," Rav Kadosh said with his eyes closed and his body swaying back and forth.

Even amidst the spectacular sight, Elisha couldn't help thinking that it was annoying how Rav Kadosh always seemed to read his mind. Why wasn't he reading Aaron's mind? That would probably be more interesting, but then he realized that if Rav Kadosh was reading his mind *now*, he better stop thinking all together. Suddenly, the room became pitch black. Elisha waited a second before letting out a timid, "hello?"

"Silence!" Rav Kadosh commanded.

Elisha waited in the thick darkness, growing more scared every second. Maybe he had turned blind from looking at the too bright symbols? He had to say something, and it burst out almost on its own. "*I can't see!*" He almost said it again when the room lit up again with the fiery symbols, but now only *one* string of symbols was in the prism-colored lightning. All the rest had turned a vivid fiery black that flashed in negative whenever you blinked. It hurt to look at the black ones, they were too intensely bright and there was something dark and threatening looking about them. Rav Kadosh immediately took the Ispaklaria key out of Elisha's hands and started rotating the Choshen stone in the middle, but as hard as he tried, it wasn't moving. Rav Kadosh adjusted his round rimless glasses more than once and then tilted his head to the side. "Hmmm . . . this key . . . ." and he looked over his glasses at them, "did either one of you tamper with this key?"

Elisha and Aaron were nervously shaking their heads, 'no'.

"Then why is it stuck?" Rav Kadosh seemed very anxious and then started mumbling to himself through gritted teeth while exerting all his strength to rotate the stone. "Why only *one* field of vision? Strange . . . This isn't right." He suddenly looked up, stopped all his efforts and passed the Ispaklaria key into Elisha's hands and started chuckling uncontrollably, "How foolish of me. I should have realized it from the start. Someone had the good sense to childproof it!" he said and then laughed heartily some more.

While Rav Kadosh was wiping the tears from his eyes, Elisha tried ever so slightly to maneuver the angle of the silver triangle so that the rainbow symbols would make contact with the mirror stone. Rav Kadosh yelled loudly.

"What are you *doing*? *NO!* The Choshen stone belongs to the Priest of Light. It's *his*." Rav Kadosh took the triangle out of Elisha's hands and put it into Aaron's with force. Aaron looked like he had just been handed a grenade.

Rav Kadosh started guiding Aaron's unwilling arm to align the fiery rainbow field of vision onto the stone while saying, "Do not fear, my dear Kohen, the only thing to fear is your inability to *LET GO*."

Aaron was resisting, but Rav Kadosh was firm and the second the rainbow field of vision hit the stone it transformed into a rushing waterfall—except that the water was rushing up and at the same time it was reflecting the rainbow colors.

Rav Kadosh seemed thrilled and with a quick swing of his arm he blocked Elisha and moved him off to the side. "Elisha move *away* from the field of vision and only enter it when you are truly ready to receive."

He then put one hand behind his back and straightened himself as tall as he could. "Now watch," he said as he put his hand straight into the rushing water. "I do not reflect in your eyes, because I have the attribute of selflessness. And by the way there are only 36 of us on the planet."

Elisha was sure that he had just given away that Aaron was *also* one of the hidden 36. But, then why didn't he say anything about Aaron too? He was about to speak up, when Rav Kadosh quickly sensed it and cut him abruptly short.

"Do not interrupt! Pay careful attention Elisha to the reflections of the Ispaklaria. Only *you*, as the *Yessod*, will be able to see the truth. They will guide you."

Elisha quickly thought about Josh's black shadow reflection and wanted to ask, but the Rav was definitely not to be disturbed.

"You also must *never* reveal the identity of the 36— not to any living person and especially *NOT* to one of the 36 people themselves. You, my boy, are *not* one of them, and you do *not* have the attribute of selflessness." At that moment the Rav stopped and turned to stare glaringly into Elisha's eyes and asked. "Did I make myself perfectly clear?"

Elisha automatically answered, "Yes."

But the Rav General wasn't finished with him. "Is it at all necessary for me to repeat any of those 'nevers' again?"

"No."

The Rav lowered his eyes and practically bored holes straight through Elisha's head with them. Elisha did get it, and at the same time he realized that he had sealed into that stare a solemn oath to the death. The Rav seemed satisfied and went on as if reading out loud a soldier's instruction manual.

"The key to the Ispaklaria is selflessness, which is the path to achieving nothingness."

Elisha by accident said, "Huh?"

Rav Kadosh realized that he somehow had to impart a sea of knowledge using the simplest of terms and in the shortest amount of time possible. He still didn't have a clue of how the Yessod had turned out to be an ignorant

11 year old child instead of a seasoned Kabbalah master, or at the very least one of those radical Fifth Dimensional Luminaries from Professor Bezalel's Chambers. He looked up at the ceiling as if to seek divine intervention. He looked back at Elisha and said, "Not nothingness itself. A *state* of *nothingness*. There's a big difference. You see, when you are *no* thing you are above the laws of nature, but when you are *some* thing you are bound by the laws of nature. Do you understand now?"

Elisha nodded, but it still meant *nothing* to him.

Rav Kadosh was trying not to lose his patience. He tried it again differently and said quickly, "When you're *full of yourself*, you're like a block of something that's physically solid. When you're not full of yourself, you have less physical substance and then of course, the less physical you are, the less you will be bound by the laws of our physical world. Understood? So the more *selfless* you are, the easier it will be for you to be nothing. And when you are a selfless nothing, you will be able *to receive*."

Receive what? Elisha desperately wanted to ask

"However, this metal piece was formed from selflessness itself and that is why it is *the* key to receive, because you, Elisha, will never be completely selfless."

Elisha felt only slightly insulted in comparison to his rising fear mixed with excitement and he quickly blurted out, "But, what are we *supposed* to receive?"

Rav Kadosh's jaw clenched ever so slightly. "My dear boy, with an Ispaklaria the only thing you receive is WHATEVER the *Ultimate Reality* wants you to have. And that's as clear as 'reading the writing on the wall'," he said nodding to the rainbow symbols.

The Rav now took his hand out from the rushing water. Elisha fell backward in fright. It was only for a few seconds, but he knew what he saw—and it was a completely dry skeleton hand that came out of the waterfall that was actually a water-*up*. Elisha was now sure of only one thing, and that was that he absolutely didn't want to 'receive' anything if he had to go in there to get it. Aaron's eyes were slit-like and intensely soaking in the Rav's every word. "And now as you can see for yourselves, 'selflessness' is not the *only* key, if you do not want instant death. You need to be the *Yessod*, the *one who connects*." He turned to Elisha, "Remember, that's you. And, there *might* be certain selfless people who can receive holding on to your merits, such as the Priest of Light. However, my dear Kohen, until you know that for sure, I would limit your activities to what you have just observed me doing and nothing more. Leave the 'connecting' to the Yessod. Because I don't have any idea how many times even the *one who connects* can receive without either turning into a bag of bones or worse. You could end up with . . . ," Rav Kadosh stopped and seemed to be struggling again to simplify something for them, "You could end up with perpetual unconsciousness." He looked at Elisha's bewildered face, and in a very serious tone said, "That would be Sleeping Beauty syndrome to you."

Elisha giggled nervously and Rav Kadosh gave him a hard stare.

"And without any living human being that could *ever* revive you. Always test it out first and *never* more than once a day, and ONLY in morning daylight. There is a plan Elisha. There is a plan! And it's your job to figure it all out by the time you come of age."

Elisha thought he heard a chuckle, but then the Rav's voice started trembling.

"I should only merit to see it."

Elisha lowered his head. That was two years away! Was he going to have to wait *two* years to use the Ispaklaria? It seemed like it, and actually, that probably wasn't enough time to figure out how to become nothing so you could receive something.

"As with everything, you need to work . . . on your selflessness that is. The day you are truly selfless you will be able to receive alone, but until then, you will always need the Kohen of Light to guide you." Rav Kadosh bowed again in Aaron's direction and then faced him head on. "And *you* my dear Kohen are now in the unenviable position of explaining to the boy the *realities* of life, and do not look so modest. It's a subject with which I believe you have a wealth of experience, from your time spent at the Jerusalem Psychiatric Hospital."

Aaron looked like he had been hit straight into his gut and Elisha couldn't stand it anymore. He burst out his frantic question in complete desperation, "So is the Ispaklaria like some kind of portal that's going to take me to, you know, an alternate reality in a different dimension??"

Rav Kadosh turned white. "*A portal? An alternate reality!!?*" He groped for some place to sit down and landed on Elisha's messy bed and then buried his face in his hands. Aaron gave Elisha a 'now-you've-done-it' look and shifted his own gaze to the ceiling. Rav Kadosh started slowly wiping his hands down from his forehead to his neck. Then in a tone of voice that sounded unusually high pitched, he said, "Elisha my boy, come over here please. I think you haven't quite heard *every* single thing that I've just said." He patted Elisha's head gently, "I know, I know, you've watched so many science fiction movies and have played *so, SO* many video games that it's basically hopeless. But, you see my boy here's the thing. All of this," he said as he waved his hand at everything in the room. "All of *this* is a virtual reality. *This* is the illusion." He then started patting Elisha's hand reassuringly. "So, you're not *going* anywhere. You *stay* with the Ispaklaria—with the ultimate reality and *receive* while letting go of this one. And dimensions are meaningless in ultimate reality. That's the whole point!" Rav Kadosh started grumbling, "Your generation has turned *delusional* from playing all those 3D computer games. I have *no* idea how Professor Bezalel manages to squeeze an iota of wisdom into your warped minds!"

Elisha must have looked pathetic because Rav Kadosh smiled at him pitifully before shutting his eyes tight. He then abruptly faced Elisha head on with his commanding voice. "I promise you my boy, you *will* understand very soon, but for now there is no time to waste . . . Behold the night chambers of Solomon! Sixty of Israel's mightiest warriors would surround it, each with his sword drawn and they'd still shake in fear through the nights." Just as he'd finished the sentence, the mirror transformed back to its misty mirror exterior.

Elisha knew the last chant real well. He only said it every night before going to sleep. He also knew all the legends of King Solomon from Saba Gabriel, and felt suddenly terrified. One of those legends was that King Solomon couldn't even go to sleep at night without being heavily guarded because all the dark forces would come out at night to attack him when his guard was down. Elisha was wondering what it had to do with his room and the tornado snake, and was hoping there was *no* connection.

"Now Elisha, listen very carefully. You must *never* go

to sleep at night without covering the Ispaklaria. There are forces that will do everything they can to destroy you and believe me they *will* succeed on the night that you do not cover this stone."

Elisha gulped noisily. *There was a connection.* He suddenly didn't want a piece of any 'ultimate reality' in his bedroom if tornado snakes could come out of it.

"Elisha, you will sleep with this every night, as an extra safety precaution and no danger will harm you."

Rav Kadosh handed him a small folded up piece of parchment, but when he took it, all he could notice was Rav Kadosh's hand which suddenly looked like an ancient gnarled up tree. Elisha quickly looked at his face and then he saw IT again; a face that was so old and wrinkled it shouldn't even be on the planet.

Rav Kadosh lowered his head and said quickly, "And I will be unavailable until the day before the 9th of Av."

Elisha made a quick calculation, about another two and a half weeks! That seemed unbearable. In the past week, he had already desperately needed him twice. And now Elisha's head was spinning with so many millions of questions, he couldn't even think of which one to ask first. And then with no warning, there was that dreaded sentence.

"As you know, I'm not allowed to leave my post," and with that he was off.

He was off! How could he have just gone off? Aaron's expression said the same thing. Here they were, shocked out of their minds and now abandoned. They both sat down on Elisha's unmade bed at the same time. For a few seconds neither one of them could even open his mouth until Elisha suddenly jumped up.

"Wait! We forgot to ask him . . . we forgot to ask—"

"Yeah! We forgot to ask everythin' about somethin' that's nothin'?" Aaron added caustically.

"No. The letters of fire. We didn't even ask! Those symbols in the fields of vision. They must be messages that will lead us to the gifts... that was the most important thing and we didn't even ask what they meant!!" Elisha stopped himself as he looked carefully at Aaron's tired face. "Oh! *You* know, right? It's your key, so you know what those symbols mean, right?"

Aaron just coughed into his hand and scratched his forehead.

Elisha stared at him. "You mean *you* don't even know??!!

"*Hey!* Hold on a minute! I haven't decided yet if any of this really happened."

Elisha looked at him totally stunned. His eyes were so startled that Aaron felt even crazier denying it.

Elisha's whole body drooped as he moped, "We don't even *know* WHAT we're getting!"

"Will you stop saying *that*! Receivin' doesn't mean you actually 'get' somethin'. What do you think?" Aaron asked while looking at the strange object in his hands. "You think this is the key to some TOYSRUS that you just keep pullin' birthday presents out of?"

It wasn't what Elisha meant, but he still asked sarcastically, "No? Then what *does* it mean?"

"I think he meant *receivin'*," Aaron explained as he made a graceful arced movement with his hand, "like you *receive* knowledge, you know, 'gifts' of knowledge or you have one of those deep life-changin' experiences. You know, like those people who go to Tibet."

Even Elisha could tell that army field cook, hulking mover, X-beggar Aaron was *totally* out of his element on this one. He used Aaron's same hand gestures when he said,

"Really, then how *did* I '*receive*' the message to find you, the Choshen stone and how was it that I almost '*received*' a tornado snake?"

Aaron suddenly dashed out the door yelling over his shoulder, "I'm gonna get some air and maybe I can catch up with him."

At one point, Aaron was even running in circles throughout all the tiny alleyways the Rav could have possibly taken, but it was no use. It was strange because Aaron was fast on his feet, certainly faster than . . . old antique-turned-fossil-in-front-of-their-eyes, Rav Kadosh. Aaron stood for a minute trying to catch his breath. He felt a strange chill climbing up his spine. Maybe he *had* been right. He couldn't find Rav Kadosh because . . . he had never really been to the house to begin with. But Aaron knew that's *not* what it was. It was because he had found something else. It was that creepy sensation of hope again.

He returned to Elisha's room still slightly out of breath and with a face that said failure all over it, but Elisha was too busy on the Internet to notice. He had already entered seven different spellings for Ispaklaria and no matches were found.

"You know what drives me crazy? It's that I know exactly *who* would know besides him. It's Professor Bezalel. I know he'd know in a second, in less than a second."

"So what are we waitin' for? Let's go to him," Aaron said as he shoved Elisha to the side to try his hand at spelling the strange word and asked, "Why are you askin' in English?"

"It's called searching, and 'cause it's not a Hebrew

word, I never heard of it."

"And your 10 year old vocabulary is so complete, huh?"

"I'm almost 11."

Aaron ignored him and fumbled with the keyboard, "Come on, help me out here and switch languages."

Elisha did and Aaron started typing out אספקלריה at such a painfully slow speed that Elisha took over again. This time several matches came up, and there was more than one definition. In Greek it simply meant a mirror, but in Hebrew there were several more. It could be a reflection of your heart and soul, a window hewn from translucent stone, or a window of prophecy.

Elisha moped, "No wall cracks, no ultimate reality, no nothing! None of these are the right ones! And now we'll *never* figure out what those symbols mean."

Aaron stared much longer than Elisha at the definitions on the screen and then said, "Come on, I'll go with you."

"Where?"

"To that professor . . . Professor Bezalel."

Elisha continued to brood. "We can't. He's in the hospital."

"*So?* We'll go to the hospital."

"No, he's in there with amnesia, and believe me, he doesn't even remember his own name." He suddenly turned to Aaron and in an accusatory tone said, "But, Rav Kadosh said *you* were the one who was going to teach me about reality. So what *is* ultimate reality?"

Aaron ignored him. *Good question.* "Right, that Temple Institute Director, I heard about him. Was he good with decodin' ancient symbols?"

"Are you kidding? He *knew* everything."

But Aaron wouldn't accept defeat. There was surely some other expert around and probably within walking distance. This was the heart of ancient Jerusalem, and one of the streets in the Jewish Quarter was even called 'Kabbalah Masters' Street.

"Wait! I've got it," Aaron said raising his hand straight into the air.

Elisha waited with anticipation but was utterly disappointed when he heard the idea.

"We're goin' to your father's library. He'll have the answers."

All Elisha could think was that it was a really . . . bad . . . idea. He rolled his eyes and exhaled noisily.

"Hey, as the newest employee of the 'Hebrew Literature Archives Institute', I can tell ya that this is *right* up their alley. This is what they do there all day. They rummage through ancient manuscripts written in mumbo jumbo and figure 'em out."

Elisha knew that was true . . . and yeah, his father was a genius and a linguist, but Aaron just *didn't* understand that there was *no* way they could ever share any of this with *his* father. Mr. Analytical didn't like *anything* out of the ordinary. Aaron sensed his reluctance.

"Don't worry Elisha, he'll never figure it out. I'm just going to give him the symbols. You know, I'll just tell him that . . . that it's for one of my own research projects."

Elisha crinkled his mouth. *Yeah right.* Aaron didn't look like the type that ever researched *anything.* He sat down on the bed as he watched Aaron put on two pairs of sunglasses and then started drawing the strange symbols onto a piece of white paper. Even that he did awkwardly, and then Elisha noticed it was because he was a lefty. It was a painstakingly long process that was taking forever.

At one point, after Aaron announced that he had finished one side of the triangle, he sent Elisha to search the house for as many sunglasses as he could find. Elisha came back with three more pairs.

Aaron put all three on top of the ones he was already wearing and said, "I think I see eyes. I think those little openin's where the letters are comin' out are eyes. Maybe that's how they're fields of vision."

Elisha just ignored him. He didn't want to hear anything else weird today and he couldn't help noticing that his own legs were shaking up and down nervously. He knew what it was and it wasn't impatience or even being scared out of his mind at the thought of sharing his room with 'ultimate reality'. It was because he was intensely worried that his father would become highly suspicious.

CHAPTER 9

Fantastic Get-aways

Jonathan had entered Dr. Brody's office full of enthusiasm to get started right away. He had already positioned himself comfortably on the sofa signaling that he was ready to begin and he called out a new Chamber Seven date to Dr. Brody.

Dr. Brody was studying something on his screen. He had every intention of inducing Jonathan today, simply because Jonathan was always much more vulnerable *after* he had been hypnotized. With his defenses down it would be much easier for Dr. Brody to drop his bombshell, much easier for Dr. Brody that is.

Jonathan went under easily and Dr. Brody quickly returned to his laptop wondering which exclusive and exotic destination to go to this summer. The Wakaya Club and Spa in Fiji? The Blue Lagoon in Iceland? It had the world's largest geothermal pool. Or there was Isla de Vieques, Puerto Rico . . . .

He could hear Jonathan babbling in the background something about eyes and wings, but now he felt utterly bored with Jonathan's imaginary fantasy world. He berated himself again, wondering why he had *ever* given the slightest attention to the outlandish accusation that

Jonathan's memory had been wiped away by a school principal and teacher! And just the thought that he had nearly let a megalomaniac destroy his sterling reputation made his search even more crucial.

Jonathan was ranting something about voices and waves. That reminded him, maybe Santorini in Greece. No, it was too close to home.

The 'short version' chanting began and Dr. Brody looked at his watch. *That should give me at least ten minutes of uninterrupted fact finding time.* The Singita Lebombo Safari in South Africa was tempting, but he had already done that two years ago. Maybe Vietnam or Cambodia, hmm . . . no, maybe it was his age, but it rang of war and napalm. Now, *what* was he screaming about?

"Enoch is Metatron, I can see him . . . I can see . . . fire . . . he'll burn me . . . alive . . . on THAT day . . . burn me to death!"

What a noisy nuisance! Dr. Brody begrudgingly refocused his attention back onto Jonathan. He was beginning to suspect that the young man was tottering quite close to the edge. He didn't envy his situation, although he definitely envied his good looks. Dr. Brody never saw his secretaries as helpful as when Jonathan Marks walked into the office. They'd probably lynch him for this one. None of that mattered. He got up from his desk, and took a chair at Jonathan's side. It was a good time to make an early end of the session, and to refer him to an excellent psychiatrist.

Dr. Brody, tried to break the hypnotic trance, but for some reason Jonathan wasn't snapping out of it. He seemed to be gripped with fear as he shouted, *"Enoch, Metatron, death, Enoch, Metatron, death."* And then Dr. Brody watched as Jonathan gritted his teeth and tensed his whole body and yelled out,

"I must be forced to remember. *FORCE ME!!*"

It took three more attempts to get Jonathan back to himself. Dr. Brody looked at him with some concern. He was sweating profusely, and yes, seemed very vulnerable. *Good. Reality check time.* Dr. Brody inhaled and exhaled calmly.

"Jonathan did you ever call *Professor Bezalel* by the name of Enoch Metatron?" Dr. Brody asked his springboard question innocently and then studied Jonathan's face.

Jonathan's expression remained unchanged, but it didn't matter. It was clear in his eyes, and it was something of major proportions, although Dr. Brody suspected that it was from hearing the two strange names rather than hearing Professor Bezalel's.

Jonathan responded with a very cool, "No. *Never.*" He rubbed his eyes and muttered something that sounded like, "Metatron? No. You want to know who he is? He's the #2, the CEO of the universe."

Right, that couldn't possibly be what he said . . . Dr. Brody quickly shifted the conversation back to the real world. "Now as for *Professor Bezalel*, some important information has come to my attention."

Jonathan got to his feet quickly, and Dr. Brody clearly sensed that he was being dismissed, even though it was his own office.

"Just give me the recording Dr. Brody."

Dr. Brody was happy to see that he hit a nerve. He reached over to his recorder but then realized that he hadn't hit 'record'. *Oops.* Who knows, it might have even been subconscious.

Jonathan was furious. He gave Dr. Brody an ice cold

stare and threatened in a dark voice, "Then you will have to tell me what transpired *word* for *word*."

Dr. Brody broke his eye contact with Jonathan. He almost felt compelled to do exactly what Jonathan had asked and stupidly repeat the two words he remembered from the session—the two strange names and oh yes that Jonathan could be expected to be burned alive at some future encounter with this Enoch Metatron—not a very astute thing to repeat to an unstable patient, especially when he didn't even hear it in context. Dr. Brody quickly shifted his gaze to the wall behind Jonathan where his diplomas were hanging in expensive and lovely gold gilded frames. He instantly regained his confidence.

Jonathan didn't need to turn around to see what Dr. Brody was looking at. He knew all of Dr. Brody's diplomas by heart. He especially liked the one from Yale University that had the Urim V'Tumim logo with the misleading Latin translation of 'Light and Truth'. He wondered if the Ivy League doctor had ever given more than a nanosecond of thought as to why his alma mater had chosen it as their insignia. And he was losing his patience waiting for Dr. Brody to speak up.

"I do *not* appreciate threats Jonathan. In fact, I will not tolerate them in any shape or form. And as for your *request*, I'm sorry to disappoint you, but at my age and having never been in possession of a prodigious memory, that would be a total impossibility."

Jonathan was making frantic calculations in his own mind. He couldn't afford to push Dr. Brody off of his case. He still needed him. He *still* didn't have the permutations to access the Foundation Vault. He must have chosen the *wrong* dates. He shouldn't have gone chronologically from the 17th of Tammuz to the 9th of Av. He should have done it in reverse and as he quickly tried to grab at some of Dr. Brody's memory, all he got was a barrage of vacation resorts! Here he was paying the man a fortune and he wasn't even listening to him! Jonathan instantly took a hold of himself and realized that he would have to put up with whatever couch potato garbage Dr. Brody wanted to serve up, to at least get a few more *recorded* sessions out of him. Jonathan sat back down. He took a deep breath and said with as much remorse as he could muster, "Sorry, Dr. Brody, it's been strenuous for me."

Dr. Brody was very pleased. Now was the perfect time.

"Yes, of course it has. I do *understand*. Now, as I was saying, some very important information has come to my attention regarding *Professor Bezalel* which I think sheds new light on your case."

Jonathan thought that should be a good one.

Dr. Brody was carefully observing Jonathan's face. He wanted to catch every nuance of shell shock as it transpired and slowly said, "I'm sorry to be the one to have to tell you this, but *Professor Bezalel* is in the hospital, with among other things . . . *amnesia*."

Jonathan was wondering *where* this was going and offered Dr. Brody an expectant look.

Dr. Brody had anticipated a different reaction, so he repeated the key word, "*Amnesia*."

"I know, so?"

Well that was annoying. He must be in denial, Dr. Brody thought. "Well. I'm going to make a suggestion to you. It is *only* a suggestion and I'm only asking you to consider it. It is not being forced upon you."

Get to the point, thought Jonathan.

"I think it would be a good exercise for you to visit

Professor Bezalel and see if that confrontation might . . . might elicit some of these missing memories of yours."

Dr. Brody was now asking him in the tone of talking to a two year old, "Do you think that you'd like to visit Professor Bezalel?"

Jonathan was puzzled, and although he felt drained from the session, he decided he would have to extract the real direction of where this was going from Dr. Brody's mind. He stared at Dr. Brody while trying to appear intensely interested in what he was saying. Then it took all of his control not to burst out laughing once he understood.

Actually Jonathan couldn't have been more delighted that Dr. Brody thought he had 'self-inflicted amnesia'. He had started having an uncomfortable feeling lately that he was more interested in his own case than he let on with his psychologist's poker face. And Jonathan did *not* want him *too* interested. This new development was ideal for him. Let Dr. Brody think that he was certified crazy. In any case, his suggestion wasn't only *his* good idea. Jonathan already had every intention of visiting poor pathetic Sir Sesame Street in the hospital. It was one of his Plan B's to get that last remaining and vital piece of his missing memory back.

Dr. Brody was now struggling, since Jonathan hadn't said a word. "I know how difficult this must be for you. But, you see . . . I wonder . . . if you are so convinced that he wiped away your memory, maybe, just maybe, all you need to do is simply . . . to face him."

Jonathan smiled. In any case he was heading straight to Jerusalem today after his appointment. He looked at Dr. Brody with what he hoped was a sincere expression and said, "I think it's a *great* idea. I'll even do it today."

Dr. Brody was left chewing the inside of his lip. Something was terribly *off*, and he didn't even *want* to try and analyze it. What he *wanted* to do was to check if there was a comprehensive spa package in the geothermal pool get-away.

As they reached the stone promenade leading to the Hebrew Literature Archives Institute, Elisha was surprised to catch sight of Jonathan Marks again, this time walking through the main square. Elisha tugged at Aaron's shirt. "Aaron that's you know who."

Aaron watched as Elisha shifted his eyes suspiciously in Jonathan's direction saying, "You know, *The Other*."

"The other what?" was the only thing Aaron responded.

Elisha would have to give Aaron the full story later, but for easy starters he told Aaron what he was sure *everyone* knew. "That's the journalist who hates us. You know the one that said Professor Bezalel has Jerusalem Syndrome."

The last words had barely gotten out of Elisha's mouth and in a second he could see that he had said something wrong, *again*. Aaron leaned his huge frame against the Jerusalem stone wall, and closed his eyes. His massive hands held both sides of his head and they were shaking. Aaron wished he would never *ever* hear those two words again in his life. He had heard them enough in the psychiatric hospital over and over as his own diagnosis. *What in the name of . . . was a 10 year old kid mentioning them for?* Elisha watched Aaron from the side, wondering how he knew Jonathan. Aaron wasn't talking, but he did seem to be shaking off whatever it was that had bothered him. Aaron just dropped that air-tight mega-metal trap door on all those unwanted memories, and snapped back to himself.

While Elisha watched total normalcy return to Aaron, he couldn't help asking, "So, you do *know* him?"

"Nope. Never saw him in my life," Aaron replied.

But, Elisha was sure Aaron was keeping some very important secrets from him, ones that he desperately wanted to just have a little glimpse of. Obviously, there was a lot more to Aaron, Priest of Light, besides even being *one* of the 36.

As they entered through the heavy double glass doors of the library, they were immediately blanketed by the muffled silence. Elisha was regretting making the trip. While he wouldn't admit it to anyone, he outright hated the library. He was the complete opposite of his father who literally seemed to suck in, breathe in, and live off of books 24/7. Elisha couldn't even stand the heavy smell of so many books at once. He felt he was being suffocated by the quiet clutter. He looked up and could see his father was sitting in his Head Librarian booth high up on the second floor terrace. There he was, all white, thin and so serious looking, with his glasses glued to his face, a book in hand and facing his screen. All Elisha could think of was *all brains and no body.* And at Elisha's age, fathers who couldn't play a good game of hardball kind of rated as nobody, and Elisha's father couldn't even follow one. Even from a distance Elisha could see his father's face brighten slightly when he noticed them enter, and that only made Elisha feel worse about their upcoming scam. There he was flagging them excitedly albeit silently from above. Up close, though, his father's expression seemed more like confusion at seeing them. His curiosity was put completely to rest once Aaron spoke up.

"Jessie, we need your help on decipherin' somethin'."

That immediately piqued his father's interest. "Well, you've come to the right place. What can I do for you?"

"A friend of mine has asked me to help him figure out this writin'," Aaron said while handing his father the piece of white paper.

Elisha's father instantly went into his role of chief librarian and researcher and studied the paper carefully. "Hmm, you've got twelve strings of symbols here. They're divided into three sections and one row has been underlined for some reason. They do look familiar, although not entirely. I think it's Star Script—a cryptic Kabbalistic alphabet, although I sense a variance. Yes. Quite a variance as a matter of fact."

Aaron and Elisha did their best not to let their jaws drop.

"Dad, can you really decode things like this?" Elisha asked sincerely.

"Believe it or not Elisha, it's quite simple, just sit back and watch how we do it these days."

Aaron and Elisha could barely hide their enthusiasm as Elisha's father quickly saved whatever he was working on and meticulously cleared his desk. He proceeded to fold their paper into thirds and then laid it on his scanner and started up a new program.

"You see, we've developed a special semiotics program specifically for identifying all types of ancient Hebrew, Judaic, and Aramaic texts and symbols and it can even translate and un-encrypt them as well. It's an invaluable tool for our work here."

His father rapidly tapped a few keys and announced, "This will only be a few seconds." And it was. His father motioned them to come closer to the screen. "Now watch carefully."

The first group of scanned symbols from the triangle were up on the screen. There was a bleep and a window came up with long text boxes inside it. They all started reading silently together.

Archive ID#: 1T/MA345861
Archive Documentation CAT#: 756/386C
Medieval Hebraic mystical/magical man-
uscripts dated 1200-1300
Estimated Period of Origin: Davidic
dynasty period — unverified
Alphabet Type: Star Script

"Yup, you see I was right," his father injected. "I actually just came across another name for this alphabet. Star Script, also known as 'Letters of Fire', apparently based on the unsubstantiated tradition that the first time this Star Script alphabet was seen, it was in the form of fire. Of course, the Talmud is replete with legends that the Torah was written with black fire engraved on white fire and transmitted in that form at Mount Sinai."

Elisha immediately started feeling dizzy but there was nowhere to sit down.

Elisha's father took no notice as he concentrated on reading the text on the screen.

Usage: Secret alphabet used on ancient
Hebrew amulets attributed to Metatron,
the highest of all the angelic princes
Form: Cryptogram
Unencrypted Translation:_

Elisha's father pointed to the line and said, "Here, pay attention now," and then started reading for them.

Three Dimensions of Nothingness:
The Illusion of Space
1. North and South
2. East and West
3. Up and Down

Aaron started searching his pockets for a pen, and Jessie stopped him.

"I'm printing it out for you."

Elisha automatically mouthed, "Wow", and thought his heart would stop even though the unencrypted translation meant nothing. At least there were words there instead of symbols, and one side of the triangle was decoded. Maybe this was the spaceless part that Rav Kadosh had said. But, how was he supposed to 'receive' directions, and what would they even do with north and south if they got them?

His father smugly responded, "Well Elisha, we're not called the Hebrew Literature Archives Institute for naught."

Mr. Davidson smiled. The first puzzle was easily cracked, but he was also stupefied as to where this text had come from. It was extremely rare, and to the best of his knowledge, it had been entirely out of circulation for over 800 years. In fact, it never was really *in* circulation, but rather used by a very cryptic group of Kabbalah masters. He turned to them both while handing Aaron the printout.

"Well, there you have it, one section down and two to go gentlemen." Mr. Davidson was also a bit surprised to see how much Elisha seemed to be enjoying the academic show. It wasn't typical of his nature, but as for the more important matter at hand, he turned to Aaron and asked, "It's very curious though, this particular alphabet, *Star Script*. I would be particularly grateful for my own work, if you could tell me *where* this text turned up?"

It only took a second for Aaron to answer. "Oh, it's from old-man Eliyahu down at the Western Wall Tunnels. You know, he's always peddlin' his latest lucky charms to unsuspectin' tourists, but I guess he just wanted me to make sure he wasn't sellin' some ancient curse this time."

Aaron laughed at his own idea, but Mr. Davidson didn't like the sound of that at all. He made it is his business to search out and collect every rare Hebrew manuscript or document that could be found, and this one might have slipped from his careful eyes. He also had never heard of an antiquities dealer called 'Old-man Eliyahu' either, and continued to probe.

"Well, where does this 'Old-man Eliyahu' gentleman source his manuscripts?"

Aaron became slightly tongue tied. "Oh. He's not like that. He's an uh, a municipal employee. You know, a street cleaner down at the Kotel. This text just probably fell out of the Wall or somethin'."

The thought of an ancient manuscript possibly falling out of the Wall after having been pulled apart and stuffed into the cracks as a prayer note was unthinkable. Of course, the municipal sweepers had their hands full just keeping up with all the notes that fell out daily, which meant it would be horrendous to try and *ever* locate it. Jessie turned to Aaron and urged him again.

"I'd appreciate if you would check with your friend where the *original* manuscript is. It's a research matter of the highest importance. I'm sure you can understand it's the heart of our work here."

There it goes thought Elisha. He just knew his father would ask *too* many questions. But now, the second group of symbols was on the screen, the one that had the string of symbols Aaron had underlined. Elisha knew it was the fiery rainbow letters. The field of vision that the key was stuck on. The text came up with the exact same origin and type, and Elisha's father read out loud the unencrypted translation for them.

```
Four Dimensions of Nothingness:
The Illusion of Time
1: 2928 3338
2: 3408 3830
3: 5766 5777
4: EIGHTH KINGDOM
```

Aaron and Elisha gaped at the screen, and then at each other, looking completely baffled.

Mr. Davidson pretended not to notice and carried on with the program. But, he had every intention of finding the original manuscript, if it existed. Jessie printed out the page and said matter-of-factly, "It seems your friend has found some sort of Kabbalistic compass or a cryptic timeline of sorts, although it's a shame that we'll never know until we find the *whole* manuscript. SO, where *is* the original?"

Aaron shifted his attention back to Mr. Davidson. "Oh, who knows? This is probably the original."

Mr. Davidson responded immediately, "Absolutely not. This piece of paper hasn't been folded for more than a day. It's standard ISO A4, 210X297, 60 grams. Not more than a year old."

Aaron used his most cheerful voice to get off the hook. "Well, then I'll certainly ask old-man Eliyahu where he got it from," he assured him.

Elisha shifted his eyes away from Aaron. It wasn't as if he hadn't *told him so*.

Mr. Davidson was opening the scanner and placing face down the last group of inscriptions for decoding. It was obvious to him that Aaron was hiding something, but having been well trained to hide his own suspicions, he changed the subject.

"You know Elisha, I saw Professor Bezalel again this morning."

Elisha knew that his father was regularly making hospital visits.

"He's doing better, but they're not going to release him so fast, even though he's recovered from his last surgery." Mr. Davidson sighed, "I wish we could get his memory back for him as easily as we can with a hard disc," and he cricked his neck and announced with confidence, "One more set to go . . . and we're done!" But then while everyone waited with their eyes glued to the screen, the word 'Unidentifiable' started crossing the screen in lightning quick movements.

"Now that's strange," said Mr. Davidson with excitement rising in his voice. "Those symbols looked just the same as the others. Let's try it one more time."

The program instantly froze, and then started to moan, and then everything blacked out. It happened all at once, the screen, the lights, the whole library was out. Elisha was sure he had seen something written on the screen before it went dead, but it was too fast for him to read. Aaron was the one who spoke up, "I caught something, did you?" But the bubble of silence in the library had been broken and a cacophony of loud disgruntled voices was rising up from the visiting public below.

Elisha's father was extremely annoyed. "Why didn't the generators kick in?" He barely finished his sentence when everything went back on again and silence immediately resettled in below them. Jessie went over to the banister and inspected his kingdom on all sides. He came back to his desk and said, "Good. They did."

The program was back on too and making a chorus of all kinds of bleeps, and skipping grinding sounds, and then the only thing the black screen produced was, *Virus detected*. Now his father was really flustered.

"Well, that can't be. That's *impossible*." He angrily hit a quick dial on his phone and spoke impatiently. "Aver—we've got a virus."

They couldn't hear the voice on the other line, but his father said, "Of course I know that it's ridiculous. How long will it take you to get here?"

Aaron and Elisha exchanged guilty looks while his father sighed in disgust as he got off the phone. But now there were two people who were suddenly invading the space of his father's terrace. Elisha looked up and saw Akiva Ra'am and Devorah Barak. Their faces seemed troubled. Akiva was in uniform, and was about to speak up, but even before he got a word out, Elisha's father asked with a knowing voice,

"You didn't *save* it before the power outage?"

They both shook their heads no.

"Great. This is outrageous. Call Menashe. He's in the archives downstairs. Maybe he can recover something," he said in an extremely aggravated voice as he waved them away.

Elisha stared as they went back down the stairs. They didn't know it, but they were both his real-life heroes. Actually, they were probably everyone else's in their neighborhood too. They were the only two who had reached the Seventh Chamber besides, of course, 'The Other'. But, more than that, Akiva was a fighter pilot in the Israeli Air Force and nothing was more amazing than that. And Devorah—well all the parents *always* liked to talk about Devorah. She had the highest IQ of anyone that had ever attended North Temple Mount Academy, but that, in Elisha's mind, wasn't important. She was the European Champion in Taekwondo and that was *really* awesome! He couldn't help positioning himself to look over the banister and watch them from the bird's eye view of the terrace while his father obsessed over the program. Devorah was of course Akiva's girlfriend. He wondered what they were supposed to save, and just then Aaron grabbed the back of Elisha's shirt to refocus his attention on the screen which seemed back to normal. His father seemed to sigh in relief as he rubbed the back of his neck in a circular motion.

"Well, gentleman, that's it! There's nothing more for you to do here now."

Aaron and Elisha were both totally disappointed.

"But Dad, it looks okay now. Can't you try it again, please, *please*?"

"No. Absolutely not. I've got to run a complete scan now."

Mr. Davidson stood up, almost pushing them out, but leaning down to Elisha he said, "I see that you've surprisingly taken an interest in one of my favorites—ancient Hebrew alphabets. I'm going to bring you home some excellent reading material." And then he turned to Aaron,

"Well, we'll be seeing you the day after tomorrow, right?"

"You bet," answered Aaron enthusiastically.

"Yes, it's exciting times. It's our largest acquisition, over 18,000 incoming books and manuscripts and maybe 18,001 if you find this one."

"What time did you want me to start workin'?" Aaron asked casually as he headed for the stairs.

"10:00am daily. You need to work alongside our archivist Menashe who unfortunately has a bad habit of getting a late start to his day."

But Mr. Davidson wasn't even looking at them anymore. He had a major clean up job ahead of him now. There was no doubt that he had actually enjoyed their little interruption. There was nothing like a nice logical code break to make him feel satisfied, and nothing more fascinating than an *undecipherable* code to get his blood pumping. It was too far-fetched by any logical possibility that his son and Aaron were trying to intentionally crash the system. He knew both their bios like the back of his hand, but all the same, the thought had crossed his lightning sharp paranoid mind before he eliminated it. All he could think of doing now was getting the program debugged so that he could figure out the last one. He would have to put out an alert on that text, but he would do it highly confidentially. Mr. Davidson actually loved the 'nobody' persona, but Elisha's father definitely wasn't a nobody. Certainly at the highest ranks of a certain non-existent department in the Israeli government, they were working very hard to keep it looking that way.

As they walked out of the library feeling like thieves, Aaron couldn't help commenting, "Seven out of twelve ain't bad at all. And you know, I even caught a glimpse of that last one that almost brought the house down."

Elisha responded, "So did I, but it was too quick. What did you see?"

"I saw 'five' for a split second," Aaron said hesitantly, "maybe fifth dimension, right? It would go with the others. Not that there is one, but I kinda think that's what I saw. And," he added, "*who* was right about your dad havin' the answers? Come on, admit it!"

Elisha wouldn't let him get away with that one. "Yeah, right! Just wait. You'll see. He's not going to leave you alone about it for the rest of your life. And it's not like we really got anywhere. Now we've got to find someone *else* to decode what we decoded because none of it made any sense."

Aaron shrugged off Elisha's concern. He was more concerned about himself. He couldn't understand why he was getting totally swept away into '*let go*' land, and couldn't even find the brakes. If he hadn't heard his own voice, he wouldn't have believed the next words that came out of his mouth.

"That's if he can find us after tomorrow mornin' . . . cause I'm thinkin' you're gonna 'receive' an ultimate reality called um," Aaron double checked the print out, "4 dimensions of nothingness. The Illusion of Time: 2928 3338 . . . our child-proofed rainbow line."

Elisha suddenly didn't like the enthusiasm Aaron had in his voice for the weird, meaningless message. "Really? Well, I kind of don't like the sound of it."

"How can you *not* like the way it sounds? You don't even know what it is?"

"That's why I don't like it. I liked the sound of that Eighth Kingdom one better."

"You kids are all the same. You always want to go to the PG13 movie," he said with a big smile.

Instead of smiling back, Elisha felt a shiver run through his whole body. Yeah, his father was the strict and boring type, but he suddenly realized that he'd still prefer his father's strong handed discipline over the thought of possibly never seeing him again or losing his mind for good. Maybe Aaron didn't have a life, but Elisha did, and ultimately, it wasn't like this reality was *so* bad. The excitement that had gripped his stomach in the library was now turning into something that felt more like food poisoning.

The windowless room was roughly circular. The ceiling was low. Its shape was the perfect place to see the reflections of the *Seraphs*—the Burning Ones, and the Messengers of Light. They were in the highest place where you could still see with your eyes. After that, your closed eyes could only see the reflections of the reflections of the Glowing Amber Ones and the likeness of the light of the *Arelim* and *Ophanim*.

Each had a beautiful name of light. There were four names that you could say every night. Michael was to the right, Gabriel was to the left, Uriel was in front, and Raphael in back. With the other names you had to be more careful. All the names almost always ended in 'El'. It was the 'El' that made each name light. Because 'El' is a name of 'The Name' that you could say. You never said 'The Name' itself. Not the short name of 'The Name', and not 'The Name' of 42 letters. Except, you could say it once every seven years after Chamber Seven, but not 'The Name' of 72 letters because that was never ever said, not ever.

There was no 'El' in her own name. She had no light in her name. Metatron didn't have 'El' either. Metatron had a higher place. He was light but also something to be careful about. The Arranger of Letters had 'El'. There were lots of somebodies in the Eighth Kingdom who put 'El' in their names. Some had the 'El' at the beginning and some had the 'El' at the end, but that didn't mean they had light in their names.

Jonathan Marks made sure that the elevator door had closed with Principal Oholiov inside it before he turned the bend of the wide staircase. Then he started walking casually through the hallway until he stopped short having recognized someone else. He turned around, and then pretended to stare at the signs as if he was just another lost and confused visitor. *Mrs. Epstein! What was she doing here? And how was she still alive?* Jonathan quickly remembered the connection. Professor Bezalel was her grandnephew-in-law or whatever they called it. He headed back to the staircase and watched as she shuffled slowly and heavily in the direction of the elevators, but then she sat down on a nearby bench. Jonathan thought she probably just needed to catch her breath before the elevator ride and he'd have to wait it out. Then she pulled out some knitting needles from her bag. *This was ridiculous.* And Jonathan had *no* idea why he was trying to avoid her and it's not like she'd even notice him if he walked right past her nose because from the look of her glasses, her prescription had tripled since he was in elementary school. And so what if she did recognize him? It wasn't like he was keeping his little visit a secret. Jonathan smiled to himself. He actually had fond memories of the old lady control freak who adored him, or rather his flawless penmanship. He shook his head. It was amazing the hold these teachers could have on you after so many years. He suddenly felt like he was 11 years old and had forgotten the note from his mother excusing him from doing his homework. He straightened his shoulders and strolled right past her. She didn't even look up from her knitting which was practically touching her glasses. He laughed at the sight and then took a deep measured breath.

The minute Jonathan entered Professor Bezalel's hospital room, a completely different instinctive emotion took hold of him. It was seething hatred, and he could feel it pumping through his entire body. He walked directly over to the hospital bed and stared straight at what was left of Professor Bezalel, his one-time mentor. But his fury instantly evaporated because the scene in front of him was worse than pathetic. He had always looked sick, but now . . . it was like he was . . . barely a shadow of a man. Jonathan couldn't help smirking. It was so ironic when you thought about it, considering the name 'Bezalel' meant 'In the Shadow of God' in Hebrew. Jonathan scanned what looked to him like a sleeping grey white corpse. Funny, the obsession *they* all had with names, well, at least the biblical Hebrew names. They attached *so* much significance to them and chose them so carefully as if it could have some kind of cosmic effect. And here was their living proof—the once great 'Shadow of God' was barely a shadow of a man, or of his former self.

A nurse purposefully entered the room. Jonathan noticed her name tag 'Bat-el'. *There it was again*—the name meant 'Daughter of God'. She smiled at him and then excused herself as she checked the intravenous. And then 'Daughter of God' asked him politely to move seats, because the doctors were about to make their rounds. Jonathan thought he might have to leave, but 'Daughter of God' apparently wanted 'Shadow of God' to have visitors, so she emphatically said, "No, please stay, it will only take a minute."

Jonathan moved to a seat against the back wall, as Dr. Yitzchak Allon, 'Laughing Oak Tree', came in with two residents at his side, one named Dr. Yael Mizrachi, 'Gazelle of the East', and Dr. Chayim Shalom, 'Life of Peace'. Jonathan was having a ball with this line of thinking. Their names were just as bad as those American Indian names like Flying Eagle or Sitting Bull. He was sure that these respectable doctors *never* told anyone what their names really meant when they were out attending international conventions. Here they were models of modern medicine and carrying around ridiculous ancestor names. Jonathan watched as doctor 'Laughing Oak Tree' shuffled some charts, while 'Gazelle of the East' threw him a smile and then wrote something in her notebook and moved on.

Jonathan returned to the bedside seat just in time to see Professor Bezalel's eyes slowly flicker open. He had planned this for days, but something about seeing the totally blank and feeble expression on Professor Bezalel's face made him hesitate—the man he had loathed so completely and even feared wasn't . . . even . . . here. Jonathan strengthened his resolve. He had his agenda to attend to and the shocking state of Professor Bezalel was simply irrelevant. He stared into the dark lifeless eyes and said in a low and menacing tone, "Hello there my dear, revered and venerated professor."

The blank look remained blank.

"I suppose you don't remember who I am," he continued. "What a shame, considering you used to say that I was a son."

Professor Bezalel had amnesia, but he hadn't lost his mind and he sensed that there was something wrong with the young man leaning towards him, but he couldn't place the source of his feelings. The woman, 'Rebecca' who said she was his wife, had re-introduced him to all his children, and this young man definitely wasn't one of them. And considering his age, he would have had to have sired this son shortly after his bar mitzvah.

Jonathan stared into his eyes and said, "Yes, you and I are *one*. That's what you *always* taught me. Which is why of course you don't have a memory now . . . You see, you stole my memory, and so now . . . you've *lost* yours."

Jonathan paused for effect, but Professor Bezalel was losing patience with this bizarre encounter. Maybe Ezra would understand what it was about. He would try to get more information for him. In a belabored voice he asked, "Considering I have no idea what you're talking about, could you please elaborate in more detail?"

Jonathan snickered. "It's really a very simple game of lost and found. Just tell your brother-in-law that I was here and it's because of what *you* did to *me* that you have amnesia. Have him restore *my* memory and then I'll return yours."

Professor Bezalel tried to raise himself up a little higher in the hospital bed, and asked, "And *who* should I tell him was here?"

"Sorry, what bad manners, I forgot that *you* forgot, even though *you* were the one who named me." Jonathan

Marks got up from his seat. He couldn't help enjoying every minute of this. Professor Bezalel seemed so disturbed and so wonderfully weak and helpless. He was asking again and again with increased frustration, "Who are you?" These little nuances of torment were much more satisfying than he even thought it would be. He headed to the door, but just before leaving, he called over his shoulder, "My name is *The Other*." Jonathan laughed so hard at the absurdity of saying it, that it almost didn't come out of his mouth. But he heard Professor Bezalel's strained and confused voice asking the empty room,

"Who other? Other *what*?"

After walking past Mrs. Epstein for the second time, Jonathan quickly composed himself. That name, 'The Other' was just so ludicrous you couldn't even say it out loud with a straight face. He snorted in disgust—*especially* because his own name 'Jonathan' actually meant 'God has given', or better yet, 'God's Gift'! He smiled to himself—certainly most of the women he knew thought so. *All* of them did, he reflected, *except* for Devorah Barak. He momentarily became flustered. She had actually dumped him for that dork Akiva. His blood almost boiled over with fury, but then he reminded himself that he would take care of that too. She would love him, 'God's Gift'. Yes, that name was much more appropriate for him than 'The Other'.

Jonathan decided to take the stairs and suddenly became miserable. Did they really think that he didn't know *why* they called him that? There was only *one other* person that he knew of that was called 'The Other'. The infamous name belonged to another Chamber Seven Graduate, except that *that other* also happened to be dead for over two thousand years. He was a Talmudic genius who had reached the highest state of empowerment and then turned into a raging heretic. It wasn't any secret. You could still find his name throughout the Talmud. Not of course his *real* name, Jonathan mused. *No.* The name obsessors actually rewrote the 6000 folio pages of the Talmud just to blot out his real name everywhere and switch it to '*The Other*'. Jonathan said the renegade's real name out loud. It was *Elisha ben Abuyah*. Funny, *he* didn't turn out remotely like his namesake, the *Prophet* Elisha. Oh well, so much for the cosmic effects of names. He was surprised North Temple Mount even accepted students with the name Elisha after that boo boo. He stopped for a minute with that thought. Elisha meant 'God Saves'. He laughed again to himself. Just imagine some kid going to America and saying 'my name is God Saves'. He'd be laughed out onto a street corner where he belonged

And then Jonathan instantly forgot everything he had been thinking about. He stopped short on the steps and stared at the exposed skin on his arms, hands and fingers, which was blistering and then starting to melt away before his very eyes. Jonathan grabbed the banister and breathed in rapidly. *Had he contracted some insane flesh eating bacteria!!* He quickly picked up his shirt with his charred hands—it was happening there too!! He started shouting out wildly for a doctor while watching his own heart and lungs catching fire through his skeleton rib cage. He collapsed to the floor in unbearable pain and then, just as quickly, all his flesh returned instantly to normal as if it had *never* happened. Jonathan groped his way onto the steps still reeling with terror and breathing heavily. *Thank God*, none of the hospital staff had heard his hysterical cries. He surely would have been committed in a moment. He inhaled deeply and rubbed all of his perfect looking skin and body and then caressed his arms. *Whatever it was—it was gone!!* He stared at his feet, trying to relax, and then stared up the blocky stairwell. Something was oddly familiar, but the fleeting thought was so remote that he couldn't ever place it. He also couldn't understand for the life of him why he still held some shadowy fear of the dying man upstairs. Jonathan sat down on the steps and closed his eyes tightly so they would stop twitching. It wasn't worth it. It wasn't worth the risk. He would have to get his memory back on his own. He stood up with renewed resolve and confidence. The fact of the matter, in his humble opinion, was that he was making excellent progress even without 'shadow man'. Certainly his memory would be returned and along with it, the torch of knowledge *would* be passed on to him. After all, he *was* the rightful heir to Professor Bezalel's work and to his absolute recollection, there wasn't a single Chamber graduate who had ever come close to Jonathan's level—a fact that Professor Bezalel had personally confirmed. Jonathan Marks was always called 'The Prodigy' of the Chambers Program before he got his *other* name. He looked up the stairwell and whispered under his breath, "Don't worry, Professor, your work will continue." He smirked to himself. *Well, not exactly in the direction you were going, of course.* There was always that gaping rift between them: 'Selflessness versus *self-empowerment*'. In any case, from the state of things upstairs, Jonathan was sure that Professor Bezalel was going to need an heir *really* soon.

The Avarshina knew that *The Other* had gone up in flames. It could see the mark. But, since *The Other* wasn't an Avarshina it didn't understand how he was still alive. It had waited patiently to understand. Now it did. *The*

Other wasn't an Avarshina, but he *was* someone else's important nest. A nest that was being protected with the last strength of a collapsing pillar of fire. A nest that belonged to the very same person that the Avarshina was patiently waiting to give its gift.

After saying goodnight to everyone, Elisha was a bit wary on entering his room. It was only the night before that the *thing* from the blood bath had come out, even though now it felt like light-years away. He reached into his pocket to pull out the folded parchment that Rav Kadosh had given him, but was instantly confused. He had pulled out *two* pieces of folded parchment. They looked exactly the same. Then he remembered that one of them was someone else's private mail, it must have been the Wall note that Aaron's cotton-candy-haired friend had given him. Well, it wasn't his fault, he'd have to read them both and figure out which one was the right one. He unfolded the first. It had a verse in Hebrew that was clearly written by a scribe. Elisha read the verse silently to himself.

> *When you pass through water, I am with you; and the rivers, they will not wash you away; when you walk through fire, you will not be singed, and no flame will burn you.*

Elisha was happy that it was something he could read and understand without putting it through a 'semiotics' program. It was a nice verse, but he was sure that it was *more* than just that. It had to be some kind of powerful Kabbalistic *kamayah*, amulet. *Or*, it wasn't. He unfolded the second small parchment. Now that was *weird*! He recognized the handwriting! He would know it anywhere . . . maybe he shouldn't have read it, but he already *was* reading it, because his name was on it! *Why* had his *mother* put a note in the *Kotel* begging that her only son Elisha wouldn't *die*!! Elisha flopped onto his bed and felt that all of the air had been knocked out of him. *What do I have??* Obviously some kind of deadly disease that no one even told him about it!! *What was it??* He saw a movie once about that, and yeah, that was it, a brain tumor! *It definitely was a brain tumor!!* He was imagining things all the time because of his brain tumor, and it had all seemed so *real, so incredibly real.* That's what brain tumors did. *That's why Aaron kept saying that none of this was happening.* No wonder he was seeing hallucinations of a strange looking Rav out of a storybook telling him he was living in a virtual reality. And if he thought about it even a second more, he'd even become crazier. He ran right out of his room and practically smashed into his mother holding up the note.

"*Mom!!* Look! *What is this??* Look at this!!" he asked shaking and practically shouting.

Tamar Davidson calmly took the small note and studied it closely.

"*Wow!* This is amazing! Where did you *get* this from?"

Elisha was confused. "The *Kotel*. It fell out of the Wall . . . why . . . *why did you put it in there*?"

She scruffed up his hair and said, "Do you know how *old* that note must be? Just look at it."

"*What??*" But, it was true; the note did look *really* old.

"I probably put that note in there what, over eight years ago, remember when you fell in the playground? I can't even imagine. How did you *ever* find it?"

"Oh," was the only thing that came out of Elisha's mouth, but he instantly felt so relieved that a goofy smile took over his whole face.

His mother scruffed up his hair again and smiled brightly back at him and then laughed. "You're fine. Relax."

Elisha did, but couldn't help asking, "But, didn't I just get stitches in my arm? It wasn't *so* bad, right?"

She hesitated, and then smiled brightly to avoid the question, "What a *crazy* coincidence." She put the note on the fridge with a magnet, kissed Elisha on the head and said, "OK, time for my perfectly healthy kid to get back into bed."

Alone in his room, Elisha carefully refolded Rav Kadosh's parchment and then wrapped it up in clear tape. He then taped it onto some string and tied it around his neck. All this was necessary again now that he didn't have a brain tumor. He made sure three times that the 'Ispaklaria' was completely covered tightly by the blanket. He wasn't going to take *any* chances. He realized that whether he liked it or not, he had been inducted as a soldier into Rav Kadosh's army and instructions weren't to be taken lightly. Then he collapsed onto his bed and let out a long deep breath. Maybe he didn't have a brain tumor, but he certainly felt like his brain was completely scrambled, that, or the first half of his summer vacation was doing a great job of making him insane. He could just imagine having a conversation with his friend Josh. 'Oh, yeah, I have an Ispaklaria in my room. You want to come over and see it? What does it do? Well . . . depending on your level of nothingness, you can reach ultimate reality. No. I have no idea what it is 'cause I haven't gotten to that level yet . . . What level am I on? Well, it goes by your age, so I'm only on level one—4 dimensions of nothingness in the illusion of time 29 million something.' Elisha blinked hard. The only thing he was supposed to do this summer was start the Chambers Program like every other normal kid at North Temple Mount Academy! He wasn't supposed to be thinking about a world without *time*, without *space*! Those were things you definitely couldn't think about for more than a few seconds without liquidating every remaining brain cell you had. He threw his tired feet up on the wall, disregarding a major 'no-no' of his mother's, while clearly seeing that his sneakers were leaving scuff marks all over the recent paint job. He smiled and assured himself it was OK because according to Rav Kadosh they were only 'virtual' scuff marks. He was exhausted and wanted to sleep so badly, but he was too wide awake with adventure adrenaline and a barrage of images started assaulting his mind, *NONE* of them making any sense. And even after all of Rav Kadosh's explanations, which weren't anything close to being good explanations, he was even *more* clueless and there was also something else he had to admit. He was *scared*. He grabbed hold of his make-shift parchment necklace. At least he could count on Rav Kadosh to make sure that nothing happened to him, *right*? Elisha closed his eyes feeling confident. Rav Kadosh did seem to know *everything*, even about something fatal that may have happened to him when he was little that he didn't even know about.

"Elisha."

Elisha stopped breathing and jumped out of bed. There wasn't a voice on the whole planet that he had wanted to hear calling his name more than that one. Without giving Rav Kadosh's instructions a second thought, he ripped the blanket off of the Ispaklaria in one fell swoop.

Tamar Davidson was nervously tapping her fingers on the kitchen table when she decided that she was going to 'tuck' her 10 year old son into bed tonight. She headed towards Elisha's room, but just before opening the door she thought she heard voices. She stopped short. It was Elisha's voice and it sounded like he was having a lively conversation with someone. Tamar certainly didn't want to invade his privacy, but on the other hand, there were times when good parenting meant having to resort to questionable behavior. She quietly pressed her ear to the solid wood door and started listening. Everything was too muffled and she couldn't make out one clear word. She crouched down onto the floor to see if the crack at the base was any better.

After two seconds in her new position, Tamar had heard more than enough. She got up as quickly and as quietly as possible, but couldn't help sighing heavily at hearing her grandfather's name.

She went back to the kitchen and stared at her own handwritten note hanging on the fridge. It was evidence. It was even more . . . It was a glaring sign. It was all coming back now for some strange reason. She *hated* having skeletons in the closet. And she was *sure* that it was because of this one that Elisha had relapsed into his fantasy world by day and was having sleeping disturbances at night. He may have been too little to remember that awful day, but his nightmares were proof that somewhere deep in his subconscious he hadn't *forgotten*. Tamar felt a stab deep in her chest. She honestly would have told Elisha years ago, it's just that . . . she was worried. She was worried that if it wasn't done properly in the right controlled atmosphere with a professional, well the trauma of re-membering an experience like that could potentially have harmful long lasting effects on a child's psyche. Tamar had seen too many bad examples of it among the special education students she cared for, and she was determined that Elisha would live a regular, totally normal, well-ad-justed life. She suddenly felt entirely frustrated and angry. If Jessie didn't find a child psychiatrist that passed his 'bar' by the end of the week, she *would*!

The room was roughly circular. The ceiling was low. The air was absolutely still. It was the perfect place to learn the difference between understanding and wisdom. There was a difference, a BIG difference. Understanding was what everyone did. They would show somebody a picture of something or explain something with words and then they would understand or they thought they understood even when they didn't. Wisdom was something *else*.

You could only have wisdom if you didn't fill your head with thoughts, because thoughts were things you understood. If you tried to gain wisdom with understand-ing, your mind would be swallowed up with too many pictures that you could never *understand*.

She had the wisdom *and* the understanding to know that today had changed everything. She had heard the tiny pinhole being made the minute it happened. The water-*up* had made a loud booming sound that reverber-ated throughout all the supernal universes. It had made thunder sound like the whisper of a bee. That was the way the universe clapped its hands.

Here, in her windowless room, everything was ready. And that's how things were meant to be. The wisdom was written long ago. She knew. *After the Temple was destroyed, vision was taken away from the world and given to the insane and children.* None of the people who were 'really something' understood why it wasn't given to them instead. They were too busy: Busy doing anything, and making sure there weren't any pinholes, and thinking that the busier they were, the more it would prove that everything was real. But that's not why they didn't get it. They didn't get it because they were scared of it and *didn't want it.* Insane people and children were almost the same because of one little thing—they didn't have the understanding *not* to want it. But that's *not* the reason why they got it. They got it because they were the world's *safest hiding places.* And now that they had made a pinhole together, there would also be something *very* important to hide.

PALEO-HEBREW ALPHABET TABLE

NAME OF LETTER	HEBREW (ASHURITE)	PALEO-HEBREW (IVRI)	SOUND
ALEPH	א	𐤀	A
BEIT	ב	𐤁	B/V
GIMEL	ג	𐤂	G
DALET	ד	𐤃	D
HEH	ה	𐤄	H
VAV	ו	𐤅	V
ZAYIN	ז	𐤆	Z
CHET	ח	𐤇	CH
TET	ט	𐤈	T
YUD	י	𐤉	Y/I
KAF	כ	𐤊	K/CH
LAMED	ל	𐤋	L
MEM	מ	𐤌	M
NUN	נ	𐤍	N
SAMECH	ס	𐤎	S
AYIN	ע	𐤏	'A
PEH	פ	𐤐	P/F
TZADIK	צ	𐤑	TZ
KOF	ק	𐤒	K
REISH	ר	𐤓	R
SHIN	ש	𐤔	SH
TAV	ת	𐤕	T

ELISHA DAVIDSON
and the Letters of Fire
(Part One of a Trilogy)

*The following is a partial list of sources that have been used
in the writing of the Elisha Davidson Trilogy.*

1. **Torah with Rashi commentary:**
   Shemot (Exodus), *Vayikra* (Leviticus), *Bamidbar* (Numbers).

2. ***Nevi'im* (Prophets) with Rashi commentary:**
   Melachim I & II (Kings I & II), *Yirmeyahu* (Jeremiah), *Yechezkel*
   (Ezekiel).

3. ***Ketuvim* (Writings) with Rashi commentary:**
   Eicha (Lamentations), *Kohelet* (Ecclesiastes), *Divrei Hayamim*
   (Chronicles).

4. **Talmud Bavli — Ein Yaakov (Legends of the Babylonian Talmud):**
   *Brachot, Shabbat, Pessachim, Yoma, Ta'anit, Megillah, Chagigah,
   Sotah, Gittin, Kiddushin, Bava Batra, Sanhedrin, Avodah Zarah,
   Menachot, Chullin.*

5. ***Midrash Rabbah***

6. ***Mishkney Elyon*** (Secrets of the Future Temple),
   Rabbi Moshe Chaim Luzzatto, translated by Rabbi Avraham
   Greenbaum, 1999.

7. **The Western Wall Tunnels: Touching the Stones of our Heritage,**
   Dan Bahat, 2002.

8. **Carta's Illustrated Encyclopedia of The Holy Temple in Jerusalem,**
   Israel Ariel and Chaim Richman, 2005.

9. **Sefer Yetzirah (The Book of Creation: In Theory and Practice),**
   translation and commentary by Rabbi Aryeh Kaplan, 1997.

10. **Meditation and the Kabbalah,** Rabbi Aryeh Kaplan, 1985.

11. **Meditation and the Bible,** Rabbi Aryeh Kaplan, 1988.

12. **Jewish Meditation: A Practical Guide,** Rabbi Aryeh Kaplan, 1995.

13. **Seeing God,** Rabbi David Aaron, 2001.

14. **Mysterious Creatures,** Nosson Slifkin, 2003.

Author's Biography

Rhonda Attar (nee Antelman) was born and educated in the U.S. (M.S. TV/Radio) and made Aliyah to Israel where she became a leading figure in the Israeli television industry launching 10 TV channels—6 in Israel and 4 worldwide. Mrs. Attar and her husband Rabbi Meir Attar are the co-founders and directors of the Tomer Devorah Beit Knesset, 24/7 Beit Midrash, and Kolel Chatzot in Kochav Ya'akov dedicated to *V'ahavta L'rayeicha Kamocha* (Love your Neighbor like yourself).

Soon to be released in the
Elisha Davidson Trilogy:

ELISHA DAVIDSON
and the Ispaklaria

ELISHA DAVIDSON
and the Shamir